An American Leadership Forum Book

The American Leadership Forum (ALF) is a non-profit organization, national in scope, dedicated to joining and strengthening established leaders in order to serve the public good. ALF builds on the strengths of diversity and promotes collaborative problem solving within and among communities.

ALF's expanding network of five locally governed chapters provides a coordinated program that is flexible enough to fit the specific needs of each locality. These chapters serve Hartford, Connecticut; Houston/Gulf Coast, Texas; the State of Oregon; Tacoma/Pierce County, Washington; and Silicon Valley, northern California. Nationwide the program has now graduated over 850 fellows—all dynamic leaders from many sectors who are deeply committed through collaboration and cooperation to bringing positive change to their own communities, and ultimately to the nation. The ALF National office is located in Stanford, California.

Collaborative Leadership

David D. Chrislip

Carl E. Larson

Foreword by John Parr

Collaborative Leadership

How Citizens and Civic Leaders Can Make a Difference

An American Leadership Forum Book

Jossey-Bass Publishers • San Francisco

Substantial discounts on bulk quantities of Jossey-Bass books are available to corporations, professional associations, and other organizations. For details and discount information, contact the special sales department at Jossey-Bass Inc., Publishers. (415) 433–1740; Fax (415) 433–0499.

For international orders, please contact your local Paramount Publishing International office.

Manufactured in the United States of America. Nearly all Jossey-Bass books, jackets, and periodicals are printed on recycled paper that contains at least 50 percent recycled waste, including 10 percent post-consumer waste. Many of our materials are also printed with vegetable-based inks; during the printing process these inks emit fewer volatile organic compounds (VOCs) than petroleum-based inks. VOCs contribute to the formation of smog.

Library of Congress Cataloging-in-Publication Data

Chrislip, David D., date.
Collaborative leadership: how citizens and civic leaders can make a difference/David D. Chrislip & Carl E. Larson. — 1st ed.
p.   cm. — (The Jossey-Bass nonprofit sector series) (The Jossey-Bass public administration series)
Includes biographical references and index.
ISBN 0-7879-0003-6
1. Municipal government—United States—Citizen participation.
2. Leadership. 3. Civic leaders—United States. I. Larson, Carl E. II. Title. III. Series. IV. Series: The Jossey-Bass public administration series.
JS323.C48   1994
303.3'4—dc20   94-10751
                                                                      CIP

FIRST EDITION
HB Printing   10 9 8 7 6 5 4 3 2 1   Code 9473

A joint publication in

The Jossey-Bass Nonprofit Sector Series

and

The Jossey-Bass Public Administration Series

Contents

Foreword

Collaborative Leadership: How Citizens and Civic Leaders Can Make a Difference provides insight into and answers to three major challenges facing communities: how to deal with complex issues, how to engage frustrated and angry citizens, and how elected officials and other civic leaders can generate the civic will to break legislative and bureaucratic gridlock.

This is a time of rapid change in communities around the world. That change may be easiest to see in such areas as Eastern Europe, Central Asia, and South Africa, but it is also clearly happening in the United States. Never in our history have there been more massive demographic changes, greater differences in socioeconomic well-being, and such alarming environmental and social challenges. And never before has there been such a lack of confidence in the ability of our leaders and institutions to address these challenges.

It is strange, given the calls for our society to deal more effectively with the problems facing our communities, that there has not been more research into and books about what works in addressing complex public issues. There are numerous books dealing with that issue in the private sector—books highlighting creative leadership, team building, communication, and a flatter, process-oriented organizational structure as ways to become more profitable. There are also books, such as *Reinventing Government* (Osborne and Gaebler, 1992), that focus on how governments can be more customer-oriented and thus restore the public's trust. This book is different. It is one of the first in-depth studies of what it takes to have success in communities. Rather than looking at citizens as customers or at building more effective organizations, *Collaborative Leadership* explores how citizens and governments can work together to address the most pressing problems in America's cities and regions.

The authors also demonstrate that the results of collaboration extend far beyond the particular concern it was designed to address. In a recently published study, *Making Democracy Work,* Harvard political scientist Robert Putnam asks, "Why do some democratic governments succeed, while others fail?" (1993, p. 3). The results of his "voyage of discovery" surprised even Putnam. The determinant of success, he found in his research, could be summed up in one simple axiom: civics matters. Adapting a familiar economic principle to community governance, Putnam suggests that the currency of a healthy civic community is "social capital," defined as the networks and norms of trust and reciprocity that facilitate coordination and cooperation for mutual benefit. Initiating and sustaining successful collaborative initiatives, as David Chrislip and Carl Larson discovered in their research, is one of the key ways communities can develop "social capital" (or a strong "civic infrastructure," as we call it at the National Civic League).

This book, *Collaborative Leadership,* is especially important for two groups of people: citizens who feel frustrated, angry, and shut out of politics as usual and elected officials who find their ability to lead hamstrung by narrowly focused interest groups and influential power players.

Richard Harwood, in *Citizens and Politics* (1991), claims that American citizens are not apathetic about public life; rather, they are frustrated and angry—frustrated because they do not know how to effectively participate and angry because they feel shut out from decision-making processes. Chrislip and Larson show how citizens from anywhere in the community can be catalysts for bringing together stakeholders from all sectors to collaboratively address public concerns.

Collaborative Leadership also has a clear message for elected officials: do not fear or fight citizen involvement in public policy making; instead, encourage it. This book gives documented proof that the involvement of citizens and civic leaders expands the power of elected officials to get things done and to break legislative and bureaucratic gridlock. Not only does it provide proof; it tells how elected officials can be a catalyst for real change by turning the work of the community back to the community.

The importance of this book should not be underestimated. In no other book will citizens and civic leaders find such a wealth of examples about how their counterparts in other cities have made a difference. The authors describe businesspeople, community activists, educators, parents, and politicians who have taken new leadership roles to help others in their communities work together and achieve results. The authors also provide a framework for initiating, designing, and implementing collaborative efforts; and they uncover the principles of a different kind of leadership that promotes and sustains collaboration.

Collaboration is a critical concept as we begin to revitalize the "civic infrastructure" of America's communities. Good examples of successful efforts abound in our country. We need to make them the rule rather than the exception as we look to the future. This book can help.

Positive change can occur when people with different perspectives are organized into groups in which everyone is regarded as a peer. There must be a high level of involvement, a clear purpose, adequate resources, and the power to decide and implement. Leaders must be willing to promote and facilitate these new processes.

That communities must look inward for the incentive and capacity to change is a lesson learned painfully over the past thirty years. It is also a lesson that the Clinton Administration and state, local, and community leaders must summon up the courage to apply. There is no better guide for how to do this than this book.

Denver, Colorado
July 1994

John Parr
President
National Civic League

Preface

Collaborative Leadership is about how citizens and civic leaders can make a difference in addressing the most pressing public challenges in their communities.

Citizens across the country are frustrated by the inability of elected leaders and paternalistic civic leaders to address the shared concerns of the community. The people of Hartford, Connecticut, for example, are no exception. A host of formidable problems confront this once prosperous city. Its economy is in decline. The crime rate is rising. Health care for children is expensive and limited, while the city's infant mortality and premature birth rates are among the highest in the country. The economic disparity between Hartford's inner city and its prosperous suburbs is growing. The educational system is largely segregated and plagued by rising dropout rates and inconsistent quality.

No single group is responsible for these conditions. A leadership vacuum has existed for years in Hartford, and little progress has been made in meeting the city's many challenges. In the 1960s and 1970s, a small group of corporate chief executives known as the "bishops" were able to control the community agenda. They were public-spirited men committed to the well-being of the city. But in the 1970s, Hartford's population demographics changed significantly as the proportion of African-American and Hispanic citizens grew. At the same time, many grass-roots groups representing minority and neighborhood interests came to power using confrontational tactics. The result was gridlock. Neither the "bishops"

nor the grass-roots groups had the power to move forward unilaterally. "Hartford is a city without a vision of what it should be," said
Tom Condon, a veteran reporter at the *Hartford Courant* (1991a,
p. 2). "Hartford's got as many assets as any place," said a consultant
who has worked with Hartford. "The question is whether they can
be brought together" (Condon, 1991b, p. 10).

Most American communities face similar challenges. Some are
making progress in addressing them. When they do, citizens and
civic leaders are serving in new and significant leadership roles that
bring together citizens to solve problems themselves. Bill Clinton
won the 1992 presidential election in part because he recognized
this important role for citizens. In his victory speech, he called for
a "new spirit of community" in America. Acknowledging what others have done, he asked all citizens to recognize that "we are all in
this together" and that we are collectively responsible for addressing the nation's problems. He pledged to reinvent government in
ways that would empower communities. He also asked citizens and
civic leaders to take leadership roles when governments cannot or
will not provide the necessary initiative.

Our book explores ways for both citizens and elected leaders to
initiate, facilitate, and sustain collaborative initiatives that can
achieve success in dealing with the most pressing community and
public issues.

Background of the Book

In 1989 we were asked to conduct a formal evaluation of the American Leadership Forum (ALF), a community leadership development program that will be described in more detail later in this
book. We decided that one part of the evaluation should involve a
comparison of ALF with the "best practices" of collaborative leadership. We wanted to know if ALF was preparing participants in
ways that reflected the principles of collaborative leadership at its
best. Unfortunately, we quickly discovered that we could find no

research (at least, none of sufficient depth and scope) that would serve this purpose. In other words, we did not think we knew enough about collaborative leadership to judge whether ALF's program was working or not. We also knew that an incredible number of collaborative efforts were going on in this country despite the dearth of systemic knowledge about how to succeed.

In order to discover the keys to successful collaboration and the principles of leadership that sustain it, we decided to study a number of exemplary cases of collaboration in communities. We felt that this research would lead us to reliable, consistent features of collaboration and the principles of collaborative leadership. What we discovered is presented in this book.

Audience

We want this book to be helpful to two broad groups of people. First, we want to help citizens and civic leaders who want to achieve a worthwhile public goal and who recognize the need for the active involvement of many others in achieving that goal. We want to help those who will lead and participate in collaborative initiatives to address public concerns. We want to provide them with the knowledge about how to initiate, facilitate, and sustain collaboration in the public arena. Second, we want to help scholars and reflective practitioners who are trying to understand this very complex social process. Particularly, we want to shed light on the leadership practices that support collaboration.

Overview of the Contents

The book is organized in three parts. In the first part, we explore the rapid growth in collaboration as a means for creating useful change and then address the reasons for this growth.

Chapter One explores the growing use of collaboration in a number of arenas, the need for a new, collaborative civic culture to ensure the success of America's communities and regions, and the underlying premise that makes collaboration work.

Chapter Two examines the conditions that make leadership difficult in America's cities and regions. The depth and complexity of these conditions make it extremely difficult to address public problems of shared concern in traditional ways.

One response to these conditions has been an increasing number of collaborative initiatives in which governments are partners with, rather than leaders of, other community stakeholders. The recent evolution of these approaches has created a need for a better understanding of what leads to success in collaborative endeavors.

In the second part, we look at the lessons of experience with collaboration in action. We explore how citizens and civic leaders can set up collaborative initiatives for success, create a constituency for change, promote and sustain collaboration, and get results by working together.

In Chapter Three, we review our approach to the research and describe the exemplary cases we used to develop the characteristics of successful collaboration. We present our findings in the conclusion of the chapter.

In Chapter Four, we present tools and concepts for setting up collaborative initiatives for success. Because each community and its challenges are different, successful collaborative initiatives must be designed to specifically respond to a particular situation. No two initiatives are alike.

In Chapter Five, we see how citizens and civic leaders can initiate a collaborative project. They create a constituency for change by building broad-based involvement, creating a credible, open process, soliciting the commitment of visible, acknowledged leaders, and gaining the support or acquiescence of "established" authorities or powers.

In Chapter Six, we talk about how collaborative leaders promote and sustain collaboration. They build trust among diverse and disparate stakeholders, actively promote and safeguard the collaborative process, and push the common goal. By shepherding the collaborative process, they allow citizens to collectively create shared visions and solve problems.

In Chapter Seven, we find out that successful collaboration leads to much more than tangible results. It also empowers citizens and, in many cases, changes the way communities do business on public issues. It begins to create a new civic culture and a deeper sense of connectedness and community.

Part Three begins with the principles of collaborative leadership that emerged from our research and concludes with a new vision of civic action.

In Chapter Eight, we present the principles of collaborative leadership. As we found, collaborative leaders take a very different approach to leadership, rejecting the more traditional tactical and positional approaches.

In Chapter Nine, we present a new vision of civic action and community. Rather than deferring to governments, citizens and civic leaders are taking responsibility for solving public problems of shared concern. They recognize that despite massive public opinion supporting the need for change on most public issues, the political will to change rarely exists. Successfully addressing difficult public problems requires creating, through collaborative engagement, the civic will necessary to initiate and sustain needed change.

As we concluded our research, we began to notice a number of emerging collaborative initiatives that were designed to do more than achieve tangible results. They were designed to acknowledge a deep sense of interdependence and to seek a deeper, more intimate connection with others. In essence, the purpose of these initiatives was to create an abiding sense of community—a sense that "we are all in this together." The authors of these initiatives created this sense by confirming the value of individual citizens and affirming their membership in the broader community, building trust so that citizens can be of mutual help to each other, acknowledging a responsibility to the broader interests of the community, and learning the rituals and practices of working and living together successfully.

Finally, two appendixes are included for more traditional research purposes. Appendix A contains a discussion of the research on which this book is based. Appendix B contains an instrument for measuring the status of a collaborative effort, along with some preliminary information on reliability and validity for the measure.

A New Vision of Leadership

We learned through our research that those leaders who are most effective in addressing public issues are not necessarily the ones who know the most about the issues. Rather, they are the ones who have the credibility to get the right people together to create visions, solve problems, and reach agreements about implementable actions. They are not the leaders who tell us what to do. Instead, they are the ones who help us work together constructively. They do not work through small groups of elite positional leaders or through interest groups. On the contrary, they are deeply democratic and inclusive. They have an inherent belief that citizens can work together to address their own needs.

We also learned that this new leadership role is not the exclusive realm of highly visible, powerful leaders. Any citizen has the capacity to practice collaborative leadership. The skills and concepts can be learned, as groups such as the American Leadership Forum have demonstrated. Collaborative initiatives, when carefully conceived and designed, can begin in any part of the community through the committed work of any citizen.

Our major purpose is to convince you that there are other, more effective ways of leading than those we have traditionally practiced—ways that can help us collectively achieve our deepest desires for justice and community.

Denver, Colorado   David D. Chrislip
July 1994   Carl E. Larson

Acknowledgments

This book was inspired by Joseph Jaworski, the founding chairman of the American Leadership Forum. Joe's intuitive sense for the need for collaboration in communities and in the nation emerged many years ago. He understood that we are all connected in very deep ways and must work together if we are to have any hope for making progress on our most pressing public concerns. We appreciate both his inspiration and his persistence in the pursuit of this vision.

Through Joe's efforts, the American Leadership Forum received grants from the John D. and Catherine T. MacArthur Foundation and the Henry Luce Foundation, which allowed us to accomplish the research this book is based on. Without the support of these foundations, this book would not have been possible.

Our research was informed and illuminated by six prominent leadership theorists and practitioners: Harlan Cleveland, Ronald Heifetz, Barbara Kellerman, William McGill, John Parr, and Elsa Porter. All of them recognized the need for a greater understanding of collaboration—especially the role of leadership in collaborative endeavors.

This book was truly a collaborative endeavor, with many others helping us in numerous ways. David Straus and others from Interaction Associates introduced us to the skills and practices of collaboration. David's deep, experiential understanding of collaborative processes helped inform the direction of our research. Chris Gates and Bill Potapchuk were especially helpful in finding and selecting the cases for the research. Beth Smith worked closely with us in identifying the exemplary cases, interviewing participants, and summarizing and interpreting the findings. Alan Shrader of Jossey-Bass gave us invaluable advice about how to make the book more readable and accessible. Dean Chrislip, Mildred Chrislip, Stephen McCormick, Harry Merrow, John Parr, Catherine Sweeney, Sandra Widener, and Carol Wilson gave their time and critical attention to help us refine and sharpen the presentation of our ideas.

We thank all of you for your very special encouragement and support.

—D.D.C. and C.E.L.

The Authors

David D. Chrislip is senior associate of the National Civic League and former vice president of research and development for the American Leadership Forum. He is the co-founder of the Denver Community Leadership Forum and serves as a consultant to leaders, communities, and organizations. His work has focused on two areas: leadership development and collaboratively addressing complex community issues. His roles include research, process design, capacity building, leadership coaching and consulting, and facilitation. He teaches graduate courses in leadership and ethics at the University of Denver and at the University of Colorado, Denver. He is also senior course director with the Colorado Outward Bound School and the National Outdoor Leadership School. In 1979 he started the three-month-long Leadership Development Program at the Colorado Outward Bound School. Previously, he served in financial management positions with the Boeing Company.

An experienced seminar leader and consultant, Chrislip has worked with many communities and organizations, both nationally and internationally, and has conducted leadership development programs for several thousand students, managers, and community leaders.

Chrislip's interest in leadership and leadership development began when he directed the instructor training programs for the National Outdoor Leadership School. One of his responsibilities in that role was to decide which instructor candidates were capable of taking a group of novices into the mountains for a month or more and bringing them back safely. This task raised fundamental questions about the nature of leadership and the ability of individuals to develop or enhance their leadership capacities.

Chrislip received his B.A. degree (1966) from Oklahoma State University in economics and history, his M.S. degree (1970) from Wichita State University in economics, and his M.P.A. degree (1982) from Harvard University's John F. Kennedy School of Government.

Carl E. Larson is professor of human communication studies and past dean of social sciences at the University of Denver. He does extensive consulting with both private- and public-sector organizations on teamwork and collaboration.

Larson's main research activities have focused on groups and teams and on negotiation and collaborative processes. He has coauthored seven books on communication, including *Teamwork: What Must Go Right/What Can Go Wrong*, with Frank LaFasto, and *Successful Communication and Negotiation*, with Alvin Goldberg.

Larson received his B.A. degree (1961) in speech and drama from Idaho State University and both his M.A. degree (1962) and Ph.D. degree (1965) in communication from the University of Kansas.

Collaborative Leadership

Part One

The Case for Collaboration

Citizens and civic leaders across the country are addressing complex public issues in collaborative ways. They are taking new leadership roles that lead to new visions and strategies for meeting public needs and create a new civic culture. By creating constructive approaches to help diverse citizens with disparate interests interact, they are finding ways to meet the broader needs of the community.

Leaders and citizens in this country's cities and regions face unprecedented challenges in addressing public problems of shared concern. Despite differences in culture, place, and circumstance, these challenges are strikingly similar in terms of the political dynamics of the issues. What makes leadership difficult in one area is the same in other areas. Traditional forms of civic and political leadership have failed to cope with these challenges.

Chapter One

The Promise of Collaboration

A growing sense of anomie pervades the conventional wisdom about the role of citizens in politics. This way of thinking holds that citizens no longer care about public life. They have no sense of civic duty or public purpose. They are apathetic and have no desire to participate in public concerns. Efforts to counter this breakdown usually look no deeper than reforms designed to improve faith and participation in electoral politics. Few people take the time to listen to and understand how Americans really feel about politics and the role they want to play in public life.

A recent study conducted by Richard Harwood (1991) for the Kettering Foundation tells a very different story. Rather than being apathetic or unconcerned, citizens are angry and frustrated by politics as usual. They feel cut out of the process, unheard and unable to see how they can have any real impact on public affairs. Government is out of the reach of ordinary citizens. It does not respond to the concerns and needs of individuals, neighborhoods, or communities but to interest groups and power players. Dennis Burke of the Phoenix Futures Forum (PFF) says, "People don't see any values in their economic or political lives that relate to what they want to have in their personal lives."

But citizens desperately want to be engaged in public life. They want their views to be heard, understood, and considered. They want to have a sense that their involvement can make a difference, that the *public*, not governments or interest groups, defines the public interest. Burke, a PFF task-force member, describes the purpose of the Forum as a way to "put government and citizens intimately

---

All quotations without references are taken from interviews conducted in our research and are included with the permission of the person quoted.

in touch with each other so that one is the reflection of the other and so the government is a reflection of the kind of community the people want."

Citizens ask for forums that can provide constructive ways for them to work together with governments on common problems. They would like to have information and problem-solving opportunities that go beyond the polarization of exclusive partisan positions. They want intimate and direct contact with the issues and problems that concern them. Most of all, they want a sense of community—a sense that all of us are in this together.

There is no lack of desire in citizens to participate in public affairs. "I want to participate in my community," comments a Phoenix citizen. "I want more say in what goes on." Fed up with gridlock and impotence, citizens are creating new methods of public involvement. Faced with a paucity of formal options for engaging constructively with governments around issues of shared concern, citizens are turning to *themselves* for leadership and initiative. They are tackling difficult problems not in anarchic or antagonistic ways but in ways that reflect a new kind of democracy and sense of citizenship. It is a deeper, more intimate, and more inclusive kind of democracy—one that is more direct than representative and more consensual than majoritarian. It is a shift in the practice of democracy from hostility to civility, from advocacy to engagement, from confrontation to conversation, from debate to dialogue, and from separation to community.

This shift is happening in many places on many issues. Citizens no longer defer to elected leaders or experts. Instead, they rely on themselves, trusting in their capacity to work together and in their deep sense of commitment to each other and to their communities. These collaborative endeavors are engaging people in new ways, providing the role in public life that citizens want, getting results, empowering people, building a new civic culture, and renewing a sense of community.

Why People Work Together

There is a fascinating convergence in the effective means used to change such U.S. institutions as business, education, family and children services, and health care. From quality circles in business to collaborative decision-making committees in education, people are learning to work together. They are working together because they have to; nothing else works to solve problems or to improve performance. Phoenix businessman Frank Fiore puts it this way: "I like to say that the sixties was the 'we' decade, the seventies was the 'me' decade, the eighties [was] the 'gimme' decade, and the nineties will be the 'community' decade. We've tried everything else. I think people are beginning to realize that the other stuff doesn't work. Now we have to try something new." When nothing else works, people begin to collaborate.

Just what is collaboration? That concept, as we use it, goes beyond communication, cooperation, and coordination. As its Latin roots—*com* and *laborare*—indicate, it means "to work together." It is a mutually beneficial relationship between two or more parties who work toward common goals by sharing responsibility, authority, and accountability for achieving results. Collaboration is more than simply sharing knowledge and information (communication) and more than a relationship that helps each party achieve its own goals (cooperation and coordination). The purpose of collaboration is to create a shared vision and joint strategies to address concerns that go beyond the purview of any particular party.

Collaboration in Business

For more than thirty years, some of the United States' best-known corporations—IBM, General Motors, USX (formerly U.S. Steel), Xerox, and Kodak, for example—have been losing ground to more efficient, more innovative, and more customer-responsive international competitors. Some have resisted these pressures by seeking protection for their products, while others have pretended that their size and reputation would sustain them. Yet all of these companies are in serious trouble. They can no longer compete effectively, and their size is of little advantage.

Much of their competition comes from Japanese firms that adopted, many years ago, the ideas of W. Edwards Deming (Deming, 1986; Walton, 1991), a U.S. expert in industrial processes that produce high-quality products. Deming's ideas stood this country's management orthodoxy on its head. Instead of relying on hierarchical organizations and detailed production methods to control workers and product quality, Deming shifted the focus to the process of how employees work together to produce quality products. Rather than performing independent, repetitive, tightly circumscribed tasks, workers in his system serve as team members responsible for collaboratively designing and integrating production processes. Deming recognized that if the process for working together and solving problems was good, the quality of the product would also be good. If workers were trained in working together and in designing and evaluating work processes, and if they trusted each other, they could produce outstanding results.

Deming's ideas fed a revolution in U.S. management that led toward more participative and collaborative organizations. Today's management gurus—people such as Peter Senge, Michael Hammer, David Naylor, and George Stalk, Jr.—continue to stress organizing around work processes (instead of functions), teamwork and collaboration, and organizational learning as keys to business success (Byrne, 1992). Companies that follow some or all of these precepts—for example, Nike, General Electric, Ford, and Herman Miller—have been more successful than traditionally run firms in meeting the challenges of a highly competitive international business environment.

Collaboration in Education

Achieving meaningful reform in education has been a frustrating and often fruitless endeavor. On no other issue is there more public desire for change and less institutional or political will to create it. Each new wave of the reform movement emphasizes the need for deeper and more fundamental changes in the way we conceive of education and the way it is delivered. And with each new wave of reform, real, sustainable change seems more elusive.

Complexity is part of the problem. Every aspect of education is in need of change: the curriculum, how teachers teach, the education of teachers, the relationship of educational institutions and the community, educational governance, the role and purpose of education, and the organizational culture and management of educational institutions. But this complexity is not the biggest barrier to real change in education. Instead, that barrier is the failure to understand and practice change strategies that work.

Most education reformers focus on their own substantive ideas about what reforms should be implemented. The result is often a battle of ideas that cannot be implemented because other reformers or stakeholders block action. In *Divided Within, Besieged Without: The Politics of Education in Four American School Districts*, the Public Agenda Foundation reports that, in each of the four districts studied, "the various factions—school boards, parent groups, teachers unions, principals and administrators—were organized around narrow interests, competing to influence policy and trying to deflect initiatives adverse to their own special interests" (Farkas, 1993, p. 1). Similarly, when reforms are pushed through legislative or administrative bodies and become "mandates" to school systems, little attention is given to implementation. Resistance to change within the implementing institutions thwarts even the most laudable goals. "Wishful thinking and legislation have deservedly poor track records as tools for social betterment," claim educators

Michael Fullan and Matthew Miles in their *Phi Delta Kappan* article "Getting Reform Right" (1992, p. 752).

Growing awareness of these failures has led some educators and community members to focus more on how systemic change can be created and sustained. They recognize that implementation can succeed only if teachers, principals, parents, students, higher education institutions, and community members are involved in creating the changes. Some school systems, such as the Boulder (Colorado) Valley School District, have created school-based community teams to serve as centers for decision making and renewal. Their focus is on the educational needs of children, not the management of the schools (as is the case in most site-based management approaches). At a different level, the National Network for Educational Renewal (NNER), headquartered at the University of Washington, started in 1985 to bring together school districts and universities to simultaneously renew schools and the education of educators. In both Boulder Valley schools and NNER, the reform of education is seen as the joint responsibility of many stakeholders rather than the narrow purview of a handful of experts, administrators, or legislators. Reform is mutually created and sustained by the constructive engagement of all concerned.

Collaboration in Family and Children Services

Examples of the disintegration of the family in the United States and the impact of that disintegration on children are featured daily on the front pages of every newspaper in the country. Poverty, drugs, violence, and abuse tear neighborhoods apart and destroy the lives of children. Where families were traditionally supported by schools, churches, and the community, they now must meet the challenges of raising children with little assistance. In many places, families (or the remnants of families) are unable to adequately provide the basic necessities of food, shelter, physical safety, and economic stability for their children. Even where basic health, education, and welfare services are offered, these services and programs are too often inadequate, inaccessible, unacceptable, or misguided.

The problems with the current system of family and children services are many. *Together We Can*, a joint publication of the U.S. Department of Education and the U.S. Department of Health and Human Services, identifies four critical flaws: first, services are crisis-oriented; second, the system divides the problems of families and children into separate categories that fail to link interrelated causes and solutions; third, the system fails because of lack of functional communication among the various public and private agencies that are part of it; fourth, the system falls short because of its inability to craft comprehensive solutions to complex problems (Melaville and Blank, 1993, p. 9). What is needed, the report says, is a family-centered, comprehensive, integrated, preventive, and flexible system that improves outcomes for children and families— a system that is held accountable for those outcomes, not for the number and kind of services delivered (p. 13).

These are not objectives that can be achieved by individual agencies working separately. They can be achieved only through collaboration. Recognizing the need to work in concert, a number of communities have brought together agencies and citizens to create more effective and more comprehensive services for children. When these initiatives work, they rely on good information so that real needs are met, they engage citizens in making decisions about what services are needed and how to deliver them, and they develop the skills and trust necessary to sustain collaboration.

Collaboration in Community Health Care

From the 1930s to the 1970s, a therapeutic, treatment-oriented approach dominated policies for public health in cities. By the early 1970s, this approach had become predominantly expert-driven, highly technical, overly centralized and bureaucratic, and very costly. It also failed to respond to community needs. A growing population of poor and less advantaged people had little access to health care. An emphasis on hospital care preempted focus on primary care and prevention. Collaboration among health-care providers and the private and voluntary sectors was minimal: each institution looked after itself in the highly competitive business environment. At the same time, the overall health of communities was declining. There was no focus on the whole. "Since the 1800s, when the focus was on particular causalities, we ignored the whole," says Len Duhl, one of the founders of the Healthy City movement (1992, p. 15).

The health of cities, as many are learning, cannot solely be the responsibility of health-care institutions. "A healthier community is not something any single group—including those devoted to healthcare—can accomplish alone. The community has to do it," says the Healthcare Forum, an organization devoted to fostering healthier communities ("Creating Healthier Communities," 1993, p. 3). Following the example of the World Health Organization's Healthy Cities Project, cities and communities worldwide are creating collaborative partnerships among agencies, institutions, and citizens to understand health challenges and create more systemic and holistic responses to needs that lead to healthier cities.

These partnerships are beginning to make a difference. In South Bend, Indiana, three organizations—Memorial Health System, Michiana Community Hospital, and Planned Parenthood of North Central Indiana—have teamed up to provide an array of preventive services from family planning to dentistry for poor women and children. The partnership has its own name, Urban-Care, and has accomplished more than any one of its partners could have achieved alone.

Further west, in the Rocky Mountain region, the Colorado Trust has provided $4.9 million to develop community-based solutions to health issues in more than thirty Colorado communities. In "Choices for Colorado's Future," a comprehensive study of the trends affecting the state's future, the Trust found that Coloradans wanted to participate in local initiatives to address health and prevention issues (1992, p. 21). The Trust responded by establishing the Colorado Healthy Communities Initiative (CHCI). The goal of CHCI is to set up community-based, collaborative approaches for developing health-promotion projects. The CHCI process engages citizens from throughout the community in a year-long collaborative planning process. The citizens' task is to establish a vision for a healthy community and to create strategies for achieving it. Their purpose is to go beyond the usual focus on health as the absence of disease and address the underlying quality of life.

These responses are pragmatically driven; centralized approaches to health in cities are simply not meeting the needs of citizens. The responses are also visionary; they go beyond coordination or cooperation to create relationships of trust among diverse organizations and people who recognize the need to share responsibility and accountability for the well-being of the community as a whole.

Collaboration and the "Civic Community"

As we explored collaboration through these examples and through the exemplary cases presented in this book, we began to understand some deeper dimensions of collaboration. Collaboration is not simply another strategy or tactic or means for achieving an end. It is something broader, more encompassing, and more powerful. In its public manifestations, it is another way of doing business around public issues. By collaborating to address public concerns, citizens can and do develop a different kind of civic culture that makes their communities and regions stronger and more effective.

Robert Putnam, of Harvard's John F. Kennedy School of Government, has written an obscure but profoundly important book, *Making Democracy Work: Civic Traditions in Modern Italy* (1993). In a seemingly innocuous, thoroughly researched comparative study of the twenty governing regions of Italy created in 1970, Putnam discovered that the relative success or failure of each region was determined not by the usual measures of prosperity (such as wealth, level of education, or access to natural resources). Instead, it was determined by the degree to which trust, reciprocity, and therefore civic engagement were woven into the social fabric of the region. In short, Putnam found that success or failure depended on the extent to which "civic community" existed within the region.

The "civic community," Putnam's name for the networks and norms of civic engagement, is marked by "active participation in public affairs" and a steady focus on the public good rather than on narrower parochial ends (Putnam, 1993, p. 87). Effective "civic community" ensures political equality; citizens are peers. There is a deep sense of individual rights and of obligations to the larger community. Citizens trust each other and remain helpful and respectful even when differences arise. There are deep, mutually reinforcing civic networks and associations that regularly bring citizens together in constructive ways. His findings are unambiguous: "Civic context matters for the way institutions work. By far the most important factor in explaining good government is the degree to which social and political life in a region approximates the ideal of the civic community" (1993, p. 120).

Columnist Neal Peirce addresses similar questions in his book *Citistates*. "Across America and across the globe," he writes, "citistates are emerging as a critical focus of economic activity, of governance, of social organization for the 1990s and the century to come" (1993, p. 1). Peirce defines a citistate as a region made up of a historic center city surrounded by cities and towns characterized by social, economic, and environmental interdependence. He argues that the future economic success of the United States depends upon the ability of citistates such as Denver, Atlanta, Los Angeles, and Houston to compete with international citistates such as Hong Kong, Milan, Singapore, London, and Barcelona. He identifies three barriers facing American citistates in their battle to compete: first, the deep socioeconomic gulf between poor cities and affluent suburbs; second, physical sprawl and its damaging environmental and social consequences; and third, the inability to create effective systems of coordinated governance (p. 17).

Peirce's conclusions about how to deal with these challenges sound very much like Putnam's. If America's citistates are to succeed, they must "undergird governance with a strong civic organization" (Peirce, 1993, p. 322). The purpose of this regionwide organization would be to work "for the shared and common good over pressure from special interests and the parochial positions of fragmented local governments" (p. 322). These organizations would provide the forums for addressing the governance issues of the region, fostering the partnerships necessary for success, and engaging regional citizens in the broader issues of the citistate.

The key question underlying the work of both Putnam and Peirce is this: Can "civic community" be created? The deep historical roots of civic community found in Italy make Putnam less hopeful about creating it in places where it does not now exist. "Where norms and networks are lacking, the outlook for collective action appears bleak" (1993, p. 185). Peirce is more optimistic. He believes that citizens and civic leaders can plan for and develop civic networks and the new collaborative leadership skills necessary to address the problems and concerns of citistates. Our research leads us to share his belief.

We introduced this section by suggesting that citizens, by working together to address public concerns, could develop a different kind of civic culture that would make their communities and regions stronger and more effective. The development of "civic community," from what we have learned in our research, is an outgrowth of successful collaborative endeavors. When collaboration succeeds, new networks and norms for civic engagement are established and the primary focus of work shifts from parochial interests to the broader concerns of the community. Collaboration, as we have learned, not only achieves results in addressing such substantive issues as education, health, and children's services; it also builds "civic community."

The Collaborative Premise

Organizations, communities, and regions around the globe are searching for new, more effective ways to create and sustain needed change. In every arena, there is a powerful drive to overcome grid-lock and to allow the broader interests of the organization or community to prevail over the parochial interests that currently dominate efforts to renew and change. The means used are fundamentally different than those traditionally practiced; rather than relying on advocacy, hierarchy, exclusion, and brute power to achieve narrow ends, they rely on trust, inclusion, and constructive engagement to achieve a broader common purpose.

There is a fundamental premise—we call it the collaborative premise—that undergirds these efforts: there is a belief that *if you bring the appropriate people together in constructive ways with good information, they will create authentic visions and strategies for addressing the shared concerns of the organization or community.* Underlying this premise is an implicit trust that diverse people engaged in constructive ways and provided with the necessary information to make good decisions can be relied upon to create appropriate answers to the most pressing problems. This is a profound shift in our conception about how change is created and requires an equally profound shift in our conception of leadership. Rather than heroes who tell us what to do, we need servants to help us do the work ourselves. Our purpose in this book is first to explore the conditions that make collaboration in public life necessary and then to provide living examples in the public arena of the collaborative premise in action and the leadership practices that make it work.

Chapter Two

The Challenge to Traditional Leadership

Citizens begin to collaborate because nothing else is working to address their concerns. And nothing else is working because there are significant obstacles or barriers to change that civic and political leadership, as traditionally practiced, have failed to overcome. Collaboration must deal with these obstacles in order to be effective. For the collaborative premise to work, these barriers must be understood and fully considered when citizens attempting collaboration are identifying the people who should be involved, designing constructive ways to interact, and defining information needs.

The Challenge of Leadership

U.S. communities and regions in the 1990s bear little resemblance to their counterparts in the 1950s and early 1960s. Thirty years ago, this country's industry dominated the globe, with only the vaguest hint of impending trouble. Employment in a major corporation was assumed to be a lifetime job. The civil rights movement was in its infancy. The percentage of women in the work force was insignificant. Few people thought about the consequences of the growing nuclear power industry. Except for some individuals, the Sierra Club, and a handful of other "radical" organizations, no one was concerned with ecology and environment. Our political institutions confidently played the dominant role in dealing with local, state, and national issues. (Vietnam and Watergate were still unheard of.) The American way of life seemed secure and unchallenged, despite the threat of communism and the Soviet Union.

In the 1990s, all this is changing. The apparently stable political, cultural, and social environment of earlier years is disappearing. In its place is a radically different, inherently more complex society that offers unprecedented challenges for citizens and civic leaders. In these few short years, the challenges facing U.S. cities and regions have become so difficult that traditional forms of civic and political leadership are now unable to cope.

These changes are felt in all parts of the country. In Cleveland, Ohio, for example, the accumulation of economic changes and political failures has left the city in a perilous state. Further west, in the mountainous, arid, and sparsely populated lands of western Montana, the issues are different but the complexity of the problems is equally daunting. Let us look at each area in turn.

Cleveland, Ohio

Nestled between the Cuyahoga River and Lake Erie, Cleveland prospered in the immediate post–World War II years. Benefiting from billions of dollars in defense business, the city's growing blue-collar middle class looked forward to still brighter times; but the global transition from industrial economies to economies based on information, high technology, and services ended Cleveland's burgeoning prosperity. The city's population declined from 905,000 in 1950 to just 535,000 in 1986, as middle-class blacks and whites left for the suburbs. The area lost more than 25 percent of its manufacturing jobs to the shifting economy. Neighborhoods disintegrated amid increasing racial tension as schools were desegregated. As if this were not enough, political failures in the 1970s compounded the city's slow economic and social decline.

Running on the campaign theme "One man can make a difference," Dennis Kucinich, thirty-one years old, became the "boy mayor" of Cleveland in 1977. Kucinich survived one term as mayor. His tenure hastened Cleveland's steady decline from a thriving industrial center to a morass of social and economic decay. In that short time, the mayor and his brash, antagonistic cabinet and staff alienated the business community, hired and fired a popular, creative police chief, and ran the city into default trying to maintain control of the city-owned Municipal Light Plant. His "go it alone" tactics of confrontation with the business community and heavy-handed authoritarianism in the neighborhoods left the city divided and unable to cope with a myriad of public issues. Kucinich had demonstrated that one man can indeed make a difference.

Tired of stagnation and confrontation, the voters turned to Ohio Lieutenant Governor George Voinovich in the 1979 mayoral election. Voinovich's campaign theme was "Together we can do it." Rather than going it alone, the pro-business Voinovich wanted to establish public-private partnerships to rebuild the city. Supported by the business community and white ethnic voters, he won the election, taking 56 percent of the votes.

During the 1980s, Cleveland rebounded as the city's corporate leadership and Voinovich created Cleveland Tomorrow. This organization became a catalyst for more than $2 billion of investment in the city's downtown and waterfront areas. Cleveland's recovery marked a high point in the use of public-private partnerships as a strategy for urban renewal. Cleveland had become an attractive place for suburbanites to work, and these suburbanites enjoyed the city's cultural and recreational attractions. But, as in other cities where downtown revitalization had succeeded, Cleveland's inner-city neighborhoods continued to deteriorate.

"Downtown development has been a failure for black people," says Frank Jackson of the city council (Turque, 1991, p. 45). Though the population of the city is evenly balanced between black and white, many more blacks than whites live in the poorest parts of the city. Forty percent of the city's residents live below the poverty line. Unemployment has for years exceeded the national average. Cleveland's corporations and financial institutions pay little attention to the inner city. The education system is failing. In 1990 only 10 percent of ninth-graders passed all four subjects in the state's proficiency exams, while 40 percent of seniors had dropped out. Many attribute these failures to the school board and the bloated and unresponsive bureaucracy it has created. "The [city's] problems seem intractable—'like pulling teeth from a rhinoceros,'" says Takashi Oka, a *Christian Science Monitor* reporter (1991, p. 9).

In 1990 Michael White, a young black politician campaigning on inclusion and racial unity, won the mayor's race from the long-time city council president, George Forbes, in a hard-fought campaign. Upsetting Cleveland's traditional attachment to race-conscious politics, White wants to bring all the city's resources to work both downtown and in the neighborhoods. "You can't have a great town with only a great downtown," he says (Turque, 1991, p. 45). By focusing on education, jobs, and safety, he hopes to help all of the city's residents benefit from the community's renewal. But many doubt whether he can succeed. *Newsweek* writer Bill Turque concludes that "Cleveland will be lucky to hold its own in the '90s—consolidating gains downtown and doing what it can to staunch the bleeding in the neighborhoods" (1991, p. 45).

The Clark Fork River Basin, Montana

The Clark Fork River system drains more than 22,000 square miles as it winds through the northwestern part of Montana and then through Idaho, Canada, and Washington before emptying into the Pacific as part of the Columbia River. In Montana the pulp mills and tailing ponds of the logging and mining sites that cover the valley scar its banks. One hundred years of copper smelting by the now-defunct Anaconda Company have left dangerous levels of arsenic in the water. Deforestation erodes the banks. Sewage and industrial waste foul the river and destroy the aquatic environment. In 1989 the entire basin from Butte to Missoula became the Environmental Protection Agency's largest Superfund site. The cost to clean up the river may reach $1.5 billion.

The Salish and Kootenai Tribes rely on water from the Clark Fork River to make their reservation habitable. City dwellers from

Butte to Washington State drink water from the Clark Fork. Electricity generated by the river furnishes power for much of northwestern Montana. Diversions supply farmers with water for irrigation throughout the river basin. Tourists in Idaho fish Lake Pend Oreille, which is fed by the river.

As the farmers, loggers, tribes, cities, industrialists, utilities, outfitters, guides, and tourists are using the river, others are trying to manage it. Along the river's course, eleven federal agencies share responsibility with state and local agencies for management of the basin. No agency has enough clout to create a unified approach to managing the river system. A hodgepodge of conflicting and colliding policies has led to chaos and stalemate. The local economy, the environment, the health of citizens, and the quality of life of the region depend upon the health of the Clark Fork. "When citizens with earnest desires to improve water quality wander into the regulatory thickets of the Clark Fork basin they are bewildered at what they find," notes Peter Nielsen, executive director of the Clark Fork Coalition. "They legitimately ask, Who's in charge here? Everybody is, and nobody is" (1989, p. 11).

Why Civic Leaders Cannot Cope

As the complexity of U.S. society has increased, traditional forms of civic leadership have become impotent. Most of the leadership difficulties are caused by the fragmentation of power in this country's cities and regions: authority, responsibility, and the ability to act have become so diffuse that no one person or group can successfully address difficult issues. There are several reasons for this fragmentation.

Empowerment and the Decline of "Old Boy" Networks

Saul Alinsky's first words in his 1971 book, *Rules for Radicals*, are these: "What follows is for those who want to change the world from what it is to what they believe it should be. *The Prince* was written by Machiavelli for the Haves on how to hold power. *Rules for Radicals* is written for the Have-Nots on how to take it away" (p. 3). This handbook for organizers, and the man who wrote it, sparked the growth of "grass-roots" politics. Throughout the United States, minorities, environmentalists, unionists, neighborhoods, and other groups traditionally excluded from public decisions that affected them became legitimate players in local politics by following Alinsky's advice. Established leaders were forced to recognize these groups, because the groups now had the power to stop actions that previously would have been unopposed. Power was irreversibly dispersed from the hands of the few to many empowered interests. The "old boys" lost their hold.

Thirty years ago, most U.S. cities were controlled by a small group of influential businessmen and politicians—the "old boys." They were, as the name suggests, men; and they were white. In Hartford, as we mentioned, they were known as the "bishops"; in Houston, it was the "8F" group (after the number of the hotel suite in which they held their regular meetings). Other cities had groups with equally euphemistic names. They were small groups in which power was closely held.

The "old boys" were often the most colorful leaders in the community. And they were good men, for the most part. Their guiding ethic was similar to that of Engine Charlie Wilson (president of General Motors in the early 1950s), who suggested that what was good for General Motors was good for the country. They saw their interests as inextricably intertwined with the interests of their communities and thought their actions should be seen as representative of those broader interests. For the most part, they had their way. Now, with the growth of other power groups, their influence has waned. They still have some power in many places, but they have no more success in dealing with extremely difficult public policy issues than anyone else because they can no longer act unilaterally.

From one perspective, the dispersion of power caused by the empowerment of disenfranchised groups enhances democracy: more people affected by public policy decisions have a say in the outcome. But it also makes leadership more difficult. For one thing, there is, in communities, no prevailing hierarchy. There is no center to appeal to; no one group or organization has the authority to override other interests and act unilaterally. Yet there are many empowered interests that can say no. The result in many places is public policy "gridlock" and an unfilled need for leadership that can act effectively in the broad interest of the community.

Interest Groups and the Politics of Advocacy

One of the more troubling consequences of empowerment is the growth of special-interest advocacy groups. Numerous constituencies from all sectors have formed associations around common grievances, staking out every imaginable position on major issues. Each is convinced of the righteousness of its cause. Paranoid and hostile, they battle each other from mutually exclusive positions, their conflicting aims fragmenting power and political will. Most represent legitimate concerns, but few, unfortunately, speak for the broader interests of society. America's preeminent public philosopher, John Gardner, calls the animosity between these groups the "war of the parts against the whole" (1981, p. 19).

These groups' usual method of dealing with public issues is to advocate for particular solutions to the problems that concern them. This creates a political climate that invites polarization. Unfortunately, this approach adds little to our ability to solve complex public policy problems. Advocacy oversimplifies problems and solutions, fossilizing perceptions and turning activists into reactionaries. Public policy issues are rarely simple and straightforward; rather, they are complex, multifaceted, interdependent, systemic problems. The problems themselves resist precise definition, and solutions may be unknown. Advocacy also divides. By dividing, it limits our ability to implement solutions. With no consensus, advocacy groups focus more on stopping the others from implementing their solutions than on finding ways to solve problems.

As advocacy oversimplifies and divides, it focuses attention on parochial interests rather than on the broader good. In 1992 Oregon developed a far-reaching health-care plan that would have expanded Medicaid benefits to more than 100,000 of the state's poorest citizens. President Bush refused to grant the waiver that would have allowed the state to implement the plan. The administration said that the plan discriminated against disabled people, violating the 1990 Americans with Disabilities Act. Though the Oregon plan included measures to protect the coverage of disabled citizens, advocates of the disabled opposed the plan because its prioritizing of medical procedures might have undervalued the lives of the disabled. These advocates, along with other advocacy groups, successfully pressured the administration to block the plan's implementation. With many citizens still unable to afford adequate health care, Jean Thorne, Oregon's Medicaid director, wonders whether the disabled advocacy groups really care about anyone else: "They apparently don't care about those without, only those within. I'd like the advocacy groups for the disabled to look uninsured people in the eye and say 'We did it for your own good'" (Peirce, 1992b, p. 2).

Whereas complicated public policy issues demand engagement, enrichment of knowledge, tolerance for ambiguity, and problem solving, advocacy hides complexity behind ideology and rhetoric that inflames and divides.

The Complexity of Issues

It is not correct to say that public issues in the past were not complex. They were, although the full complexity of the issues may not have been understood or recognized. Today these complexities are part of every public policy decision; decision makers must identify the "real" problem, know of or create possible solutions, choose from a myriad of offered remedies, trade off action or inaction in one area against action or inaction in another, and understand unintended side effects. An array of issues—environmental deterioration, ineffective education, inefficient and costly health care, masses of toxic wastes, increasing crime, dissolving families—are inextricably interconnected and interdependent. Action in one area precludes or affects action in others. We have more information than we can understand. When no information exists to support a particular view, it is simply conjured up. There are many solutions—but little agreement about what the problem is. The issues are complex in terms of substance, the context in which they occur, and the political dynamics that surround them.

But it is our attitude toward this complexity that makes leadership especially difficult. At a time when we need to be willing to learn and explore, we are still taught in school to "know" the answers. Our leaders, having learned that particular lesson well, cannot admit that they do not know something. In an article entitled "Leadership's Shadow: the Dilemma of Denial," Don Michael describes how "societal problems collide, pile up and gridlock in ever more complex disarray, and the more complex and disarrayed the situation becomes, the less possible it becomes for leaders to acknowledge that this is so. For to do so would be to admit that they do not understand the complexity and, not understanding it, do not really know what to do about it" (1991, p. 69). We fail to solve our problems in part because of our inability to acknowledge and work with complexity and ambiguity—a complexity that requires us to recognize that we do not "know" what to do and must instead experiment and learn our way into solutions. "Live the questions now," the poet Rilke said. "Perhaps then, someday far in the future, you will gradually, without even noticing it, live your way into the answer" (Rilke, [1908] 1984, p. 34).

The Diffusion of Responsibility

As the perceived complexity of problems has increased, who is responsible for solving them has become more and more ambiguous. Formal changes in the responsibilities of different levels of government have caused part of the confusion. When Ronald Reagan became president in 1981, he presided over a significant change in the role of the federal government known as the "new federalism." In its new role, the federal government has foisted much of the responsibility for state and local issues onto state and local governments. This shift, made partly under the guise of pushing problems back to where they are most appropriately dealt with, also marked the beginning of a sharp decline in federal resources for use at the state and local level. In many cases, federal requirements imposed on other levels of government have not been accompanied by sufficient resources to meet mandated performance standards. Local governments strapped for financial resources have cut or eliminated generally expected social services. Competing demands for scarce resources have created hard choices and left many needs unmet.

In the Clark Fork River basin in Montana, as we noted earlier, eleven federal agencies (along with several state and local agencies) share jurisdiction for the river's management. No one agency is in charge.

One city leader in Phoenix describes city government in this way: "The streets department does not talk to the planning department. The planning department does not talk to the housing department. Nobody talks to police. Nobody talks to fire. Nobody talks to social service agencies. Everything is done in isolation and often at cross purposes." In other places, such issues as health care, air pollution, transportation, and water cross jurisdictional boundaries. Policies of one agency collide with those of others. There is no larger jurisdiction to step in and resolve the conflicts. As a result, little happens except through endless confrontation and litigation that satisfies no one.

In this "no one in charge" society, there are few forums for creating recognition of the broader needs of society and region. There is no larger vision to provide a context for decision and action. Agencies and institutions are stymied by their own "turf" problems, which preclude concerted action and starkly silhouette agencies' growing inability to cope. Our trust declines. Cynicism grows and masks our failure to cope, discouraging true care and responsible action. There is no "constituency for the whole."

A Culture of Individualism

Of all the threads that run through U.S. culture, the most pervasive and influential is that of the power and the freedom of individual achievement (Bellah and others, 1985). Glorified by Benjamin Franklin, romanticized by Walt Whitman, Henry David Thoreau, and Ralph Waldo Emerson, criticized by Alexis de Toqueville, the successful, self-reliant individual became an indelible part of the American character. The institutions and laws of the United States codified it. The geography and space of the country allowed its fulfillment. Economic growth and opportunity supported it. And for a time, though some were left behind, the United States thrived. When there were jobs to be had, space to move to, and few challenges from minority interests, there was little need for a larger view of U.S. culture.

But the virtues of what philosopher John Dewey called "rugged individualism" now seem less obvious than its failings. What happens when the problems at hand affect us all? What happens when the common good cannot be defined by the greatest good for the greatest number? Environment, education, violence, transportation, and other issues do not distinguish between rich and poor, educated or illiterate, employed or homeless. A culture of individualism provides little guidance when we are forced to make choices in common—choices that cannot be appropriately or effectively made by self-regulating economic markets or through mediation of special interests by representative democracy. Our history has not prepared us for this. These are problems that require us to face each other: we must create a broader sense of caring and responsibility, and we must recognize that we are all in this together. "The politics of keeping citizens apart cannot work for long in a place to which large numbers of people with diverse interests are equally committed," writes Mayor Daniel Kemmis of Missoula, Montana. "The only kind of politics that can work here is a politics of engagement" (1988, p. 9).

The Failure of Traditional Politics

At the same time that fragmentation of power in our cities and regions has made civic leadership increasingly difficult, a number of political failures have led to an era of monumental distrust in our political institutions. The political system we have inherited is too often limiting, unjust, and ineffective.

We live in what is ostensibly a "representative" democracy. Our role as citizens is to elect representatives to frame public policy issues, to argue the merits of alternative approaches, and to make decisions for us. The people we elect should reflect our diversity and represent our perspectives, interests, and opinions in shaping public policies. As decision makers, elected officials take credit for successes, avoid blame where possible, and are supposedly held accountable for failures by the citizens who elected them. Representative democracy is supposed to work from the highest office in the land down to the local school board. In too many cases it does not.

In education, for example, citizens and the media criticize their "representatives" as one of the major obstacles to educational reform. Conflicting political agendas among school board members (such as the clash over curriculum and teaching practices between representatives of the far right and liberal education advocates) stalemate reform efforts. One way to overcome these obstacles is to significantly increase the involvement of parents and citizens in school governance. But this is resisted because it supposedly threatens the system of representative democracy. Thomas Shannon, executive director of the National School Boards Association, believes that the mere idea of questioning the role of school boards demonstrates a "haughty contempt for the American institution of representative governance" (Peirce, 1992c, p. 2). "If school boards are going to do the job," Shannon says, "we expect them not to be undercut by advisory groups or other groups in the community" (Diegmueller, 1992, p. 8). No wonder citizens distrust their elected leaders.

This understanding of a large role for elected leaders and a limited role for citizens in public policy making has led to the failure to address difficult issues of shared concern. Our "representatives" and the governmental institutions they oversee have failed: first, they have failed to solve problems directly affecting citizens in communities; second, they have failed to prevent the growing division between haves and have-nots and between racial, cultural, and gender groups; and third, they have failed to actively engage citizens in the problems of society, even though many of us are both part of the problem and necessary for the solution.

The Failure to Solve Problems

As members of legislative bodies from school boards to Congress, elected leaders have failed to solve problems for the constituencies they represent. Skyrocketing expectations, sparked by John F. Kennedy's vision and Lyndon Johnson's "Great Society" and civil rights initiatives, now far exceed the government's ability to perform. The immensity of such national problems as the savings and loan bailout and the task of cleaning up over 1,000 hazardous waste sites with Superfund money (a potential cost of up to $750 billion) is overwhelming. Health care continues to become more costly and less accessible. Schools develop neither employees who can compete with those of other nations nor citizens who can participate responsibly in a democratic society. Gangs, violence, and drugs threaten children, families, and the elderly in urban and suburban areas as police forces struggle to cope. Water shortages, transportation breakdowns, and environmental health dangers threaten the quality of life many Americans have learned to expect. On these and other problems, innumerable examples of failed leadership confront us at all levels of government.

To better understand the nature of this problem, let us take a closer look at the example of education. One of the challenges facing education today is simply obtaining funding to meet current program needs. In Colorado, the state legislature passed the School Finance Act of 1988 to guarantee adequacy and equity in school funding for all the state's schools. General fiscal shortfalls in 1992 led to the failure of the legislature to provide funding to meet the 1988 law's requirements. The legislature explored tax options and even gambling as ways to raise funds for schooling. State Senator Jim Rizzuto describes his experience with this problem as "the most appalling process I've ever gone through [in] 10 years in the legislature. It's a true reflection of our inability to govern. The people should throw us all out of office" (Germer, 1992, p. 9). Legislators passed an interim and inadequate measure in early May of 1992. Colorado's governor, Roy Romer, called the bill "a patch-over until the real crisis" (Anderson and Gavin, 1992, p. 1).

More serious issues of systemic educational reform across the country remain bogged down not only in major funding issues such as this one but in the turf issues of school boards and administrations. School board members in Denver repeatedly challenge decisions made by the Collaborative Decision-Making Committees, instituted in all Denver schools in 1991. These committees, made

up of principals, teachers, business representatives, and parents, supposedly have broad powers to decide on curriculum and personnel
matters, but they are often hampered by board or administration
actions that conflict with their recommendations (Owens and
Kennedy, 1992, p. 9). Locked in by traditional definitions of power
and role, the school board is seen by many as the primary obstacle
to enduring change in Denver's public schools.

The Failure to Prevent the Division of Society

In 1965 Lyndon Johnson told Congress that "if we become two
people, the suburban affluent and the urban poor, each filled with
mistrust and fear for the other, . . . then we shall effectively cripple
each generation to come." As America becomes a nation with no
racial or ethnic majority, the distinctions between groups are
becoming more dramatic and the separations more profound.
Across the country, racial and ethnic groups band together to secure
identity and power. On college campuses, the politics of race and
sex divide students and faculties into racial, cultural, and gender
enclaves (D'Souza, 1991). In suburbs, successful professionals
"secede" from society by retreating to insular condominiums and
residential compounds (Reich, 1991, p. 16). Fifty cities with pop-
ulations over 100,000 are more than 50 percent African-American, Hispanic, and Asian. Detroit is the most segregated, with a 79
percent minority population. Growing economic divisions and
increasing alienation across racial and cultural lines rend the social
fabric of such U.S. cities as Los Angeles. What is most troubling
about these events is that the forces driving us apart may be
stronger than those that bind us together. "Will the melting pot
yield to the tower of Babel?" asks Arthur M. Schlesinger, Jr., in *The
Disuniting of America* (1991, p. 2).

George Bush's inability to do more than react to the 1992 Los
Angeles riots is one example of the failure of elected leaders to deal

effectively with the growing divisions of society. A caretaker president, Bush saw little need to address issues of race and poverty despite a wealth of information describing the growing divide. The *Economist* in March of 1991 described the slums in U.S. cities as "shameful," a "damning indictment of the richest country in the world" ("America's Blacks," 1991, p. 21). The magazine's warning that "America cannot afford to let down its blacks for much longer" was lost in the euphoria following the end of the Gulf War. Bush belatedly began to pick up the pieces when he hastily called a three-day retreat after the Los Angeles riots to figure out what to do about urban race and poverty problems. When Bush left office in January of 1993, there was still no response at the federal level to the problems in Los Angeles.

The Failure to Engage Citizens

Over the past two decades, ordinary Americans have felt increasingly disconnected from the political process. Now frustrated and angry, they wonder how to reestablish an effective link to a system controlled more and more by monied interests, experts, and the media. Journalist William Greider, in his book *Who Will Tell the People?* observes that democracy has become a contest for the organized economic interests in which ordinary citizens, lacking the financial resources to participate, take a backseat in the political power arena (1992, pp. 35–36). Political reforms designed to enhance the democratic process, such as certain mandatory public hearings established by legislative measures in the early 1970s, have been perverted or have become ineffectual formalities. Elections, the traditional avenue by which citizens can influence government, so diffuse the impact of voters that participation has declined steadily for more than thirty years, with the exception of an encouraging increase in 1992. Politicians with facile answers pass ambiguous legislation (for example, the liberalization of the savings and loan industry regulations in 1982), which obscures public impacts and roles for citizens in governance. Bureaucrats distance themselves from the public by hiding behind regulatory procedures or by limiting public access to decision making. Ironically, as citizens are more and more being excluded from the political process, the problems that must be addressed increasingly require their participation.

For example, after the 1992 Los Angeles riots, political scientist Lawrence Mead, writing in the *New York Times*, described the urban problems of U.S. cities as "rooted in a culture of despair beyond the reach of conventional social reform" (1992, p. A23). Large-scale federally funded programs, even when well conceived, have been inadequate. Commissions and blue-ribbon panels established in the wake of urban riots or to respond to specific aspects of the "urban crisis" have failed everywhere. Volunteer efforts, such as those celebrated by President Bush's "Points of Light" program, are limited in scope. These initiatives miss the mark because they fail to engage the people who live in the most troubled and despairing neighborhoods as key resources in the solution of their problems.

None of the responses proposed by elected officials to the problems of Los Angeles address this need for greater involvement. Former Housing and Urban Development Secretary Jack Kemp considered "empowerment" of citizens essential, but his ideas were about helping individual homeowners or small businesses; he did not address the empowerment of the larger community ("America's Blacks," 1991, p. 21). Few proponents of urban or rural development really listen to what residents say about their concerns. Fewer still involve them in decisions that affect them. No one recognizes that the capacity for renewal is rooted within the community rather than in programs or individuals. The only consensus about what to do that really matters is that of the people who live there.

The Impotence of Political Leadership

There are examples of the failure of elected leaders and governments at every level to solve problems and to engage an increasingly divided citizenry. Why has this failure occurred? In part, it grows out of the fragmentation of power that makes it difficult for anyone to lead. But the failure of political leaders is also caused by the structural and institutionalized practices of the political system itself. Some of the structures and practices of representative democracy make it almost impossible for elected leaders and the bureaucracies of government to play an effective role in addressing public problems of shared concern.

For example, political leadership may be an oxymoron. Politicians want to be elected or reelected, and so they want to be seen in as favorable a light as possible by as many people as possible. They do not want to offend anyone. They either refrain from taking positions on important issues or hide behind meaningless generalities. They wait to vote or avoid voting on legislation so that others can be blamed for failing to deal with problems. When they do introduce legislation, it is either so watered down that it is meaningless or so arcane that its real purpose is obscured. They avoid important issues requiring hard choices or trade-offs. Anyone raising difficult issues does so at the peril of being savaged by opponents. "Everyone knows what to do. We know how to do it," said former New Hampshire Senator Warren Rudman in a 1992 *Time* interview. "We're always afraid to do it" (Traver, 1992, p. 20).

The practice of developing public policies within small groups of bright people in government also leads to failure. The "best and the brightest," trained to use sophisticated decision-making tools such as cost-benefit analysis and mathematical models for risk assessment, are supposed to come up with ideal policies and programs, but their solutions are generally difficult or impossible to sell. For instance, Rhode Island voters killed the "Greenhouse Compact" in 1984 when 80 percent said no in a public referendum. This complex "industrial policy" plan, designed chiefly by business consultant Ira Magaziner, was supposed to rejuvenate Rhode Island's moribund economy, but its technocratic arguments left citizens unsure of what it meant.

Institutionalized public participation has failed to help solve problems and engage citizens. One of the purposes of the public-interest reform movement of the 1960s and early 1970s (initiated by Ralph Nader and others) was to open up public access to governmental decision making. By providing avenues for public participation, sponsors of this movement hoped that policy decisions would consider all affected interests and thus reflect the broad public interest. But the methods used to encourage participation have left citizens frustrated and intimidated. For many people, the hearings are a waste of time—a forum in which grudging officials perfunctorily fulfill their obligation to solicit public input prior to doing as they please. Public managers and strong interest groups reach decisions accommodating their own interests while ignoring public comment.

Bureaucracy impedes effective government action. Progressive, "good government" reformers of the early twentieth century encouraged the formation of bureaucracies to combat corruption. While these reforms eliminated many of the problems of partisan influence, they also impeded the ability of government to respond to changing needs and to solve problems. Procedure-bound, their legalistic responses fail to address the needs of citizens. The bureaucracies' impersonal relationship with citizens creates distrust and destroys community. Bound by rules, agencies take little responsibility beyond their prescribed duties. Regulations inhibit innovation both by citizens and by other government agencies. Jurisdictional boundaries and mandates prevent coordination and collaboration between agencies, citizens, and neighboring communities. At a time when the need for responsive, creative government has never been greater, rigid, bureaucratic forms of government limit the ability to act. The progressive, "good government" paradigm no longer works.

These flawed practices of representative democracy are further compounded by unrealistic public expectations of political leaders. Americans hold a singular belief in the potency of leaders. We look to them—the "wise men"—to solve our problems. We want them to tell us what they will do before we will elect them. Unfortunately, this creates unfulfillable expectations of leaders and, more significantly, provides an escape from responsibility for those of us not anointed as leaders. When leaders fail, we blame them rather than engaging ourselves in the difficult work of public policy problem solving. We expect quick fixes to complex problems. If all else fails, we "light out for the Territory," like Huck Finn, to escape responsibility.

A Legacy of Frustration

As this country's political and governance practices increasingly fail to solve problems and engage citizens, confidence declines. A 1990 Gallup poll commissioned by the National Civic League asked 1,025 Americans which institutions they had "a great deal" or "quite a lot" of confidence in to solve the problems facing their local communities. Only about one in five expressed confidence in any level of government to deal with those problems (Gallup, 1990, p. 4). A Kettering Foundation survey, *Citizens and Politics: A View from Main Street,* found citizens angry and frustrated with and distrustful of U.S. democratic institutions (Harwood, 1991). Though not apathetic, most Americans feel isolated and politically impotent; they see few avenues for access.

Because of this, few citizens are actively engaged in solving public problems or in changing institutionalized political practices. Only 22 percent of those polled in the Gallup survey said that they were currently involved with community problems. Robert Bellah and his colleagues found, in *The Good Society*, that most people are unwilling to question the underlying purposes and operating premises of political practices and institutions. We "allow the operations of government and the economy to go on 'over our heads,' as though we had nothing to do with them" (Bellah and others, 1991, p. 19).

These problems are deeper than campaign reforms, term limitations, and voter education programs can solve. The breakdown of old power structures and the retreat of citizens into racial, cultural, and economic interest groups has led to a civic culture of advocacy, hostility, and confrontation. In this divisive and corrosive atmosphere, public needs are not met and civic problems are not addressed. We can no longer defer to elected leaders to define and solve public problems. We need to discover a new way of interacting—a new civic culture—that helps us collectively address issues of shared concern. In order to work, this new way of interacting must be able to cope with the challenges of leadership and the failures of traditional politics. To this end, we must redefine the roles and practices of leadership for both elected leaders and citizens.

A Historical Perspective

Throughout his life, philosopher John Dewey argued the need for "participatory democracy." His political philosophy rested on two beliefs: the capacity of human beings to participate rationally and effectively in public life and the desirability and practicality of their full participation. He believed a person's capacity to participate could be nurtured in ways that support informed political action (Westbrook, 1991). Journalist Walter Lippmann, one of Dewey's most effective critics, had other views. He believed that the political judgment of ordinary people could not be trusted and that their participation in public life should therefore be limited. An intelligent, informed elite should govern on their behalf. Lippmann, one of the "democratic realists" of the 1920s and 1930s, based his views on a "realistic" assessment of democracy in action (Steel, 1980). His perspective prevailed until recent years. Now the challenges of leadership are forcing a return to Dewey's notion of participatory democracy. Ironically, this shift is driven less by the ideals that guided Dewey than by the realism that guided Lippmann.

Part Two

Leadership Strategies for Effective Collaboration

Despite growing recognition of the need to collaborate to solve public policy problems, there is a substantial gap between intention and results. In most places, leaders and citizens simply do not know how to collaborate. By exploring stories of successful collaboration, community leaders and citizens can learn to design, initiate, and sustain collaborative initiatives to address issues of shared concern in their cities and regions.

Chapter Three

Discovering the Keys to Successful Collaboration: Lessons from the Field

The need for collaboration and an increased sense of community is great—indeed, has never been greater. The challenges we face and the lingering cynicism from past political failures that confronts us must be overcome before we can move ahead. We need an unprecedented willingness to set aside narrow interests to find ways of helping each other achieve common goals. We described in Chapter One the rise of civic politics and the increased emphasis on collaboration as a means for creating useful change. In Chapter Two, we explored the tension between this new social movement and the traditional practices of civic leadership. We identified a number of ways in which traditional politics has moved away from citizen involvement in public decision making.

Now we turn to the primary purpose of this book: how citizens and civic leaders can make a difference by serving as catalysts for collaboration. We are concerned with these questions: What are the keys to successful collaborative problem solving in the public arena? What does successful collaboration look like? How does it work? What kinds of results does it produce? What leadership attitudes and behaviors promote and sustain it? We want to provide, in this chapter, some background about how we reached our conclusions. We want to share with you not so much what we think but what we discovered from others. In our research, we studied the experiences, insights, and lessons of people who had been intimately involved in collaboration. They are the experts; they are the ones who can tell us how to make collaboration work. We start with six exemplary cases.

The Exemplary Cases

With the assistance of the National Civic League, an organization familiar with civic initiatives throughout the nation, we selected six exemplary cases of successful collaboration for the first phase of this research. Our goal was to find noteworthy cases that met the following criteria:

- The collaboration produced concrete, tangible results. That is, a fundamental impact on the root cause of a problem or situation was made; the effort generated more than simply a set of activities or some structure building devoid of real impact on the problem.
- The problem was sufficiently complex that collaboration across sector lines in the community was necessary in order to impact the problem or condition.
- Significant barriers/obstacles existed that had to be overcome in addressing the issue.
- There were many and diverse stakeholders involved in the issue. It was not simply a collaboration of vested interests but addressed concerns of the community as a whole.
- There was widespread acknowledgment and recognition of the collaboration's success in dealing with the issue.

The Phoenix Futures Forum

No major city in our nation's history has experienced a growth rate that compares with that of Phoenix. Since World War II, Phoenix has grown from the 148th largest city in America to the 10th largest. Despite this growth, political decisions remained firmly in the hands of a few well-known leaders until recently. John Hall and Lou Weschler, two university professors, describe the political culture that dominated during that period: "Combined with a conservative political culture, this phenomenal demographic, economic, and geographic expansion of post–air conditioned Phoenix, led to a limited and ad hoc public policy agenda often involving the smallest possible number of participants in important public decisions" (1991, p. 136).

In 1983 citizens' perceptions that the city was in the control of a few individuals resulted in a successful campaign to establish a district-based election of city council members in place of an at-large election system. Citizens were moving in the direction of more involvement in city affairs, stronger neighborhoods, and more citizen associations.

In 1988 Mayor Goddard invited the people of Phoenix and the surrounding communities to become involved in a long-range planning process to be guided by the new Citizen Policy Committee. The project became known as the Phoenix Futures Forum and was funded by the city and several private organizations. The Forum essentially became a process—one that encouraged participation by all business, labor, religious, nonprofit, neighborhood, environmental, and educational groups, in addition to city officials. Over the two years of the Forum's work, the citywide forums, work sessions, and neighborhood forums became credible outlets for citizen concerns and visions. Somewhere between 1,500 and 3,500 citizens participated in the process.

The Forum's final report was presented to the city council in January of 1990. It provides a vision of the city in 2015, along with recommendations for achieving that vision. A Futures Forum Action Committee has been established to move the report toward implementation. Paul Johnson, then the new mayor of Phoenix, reorganized the city council subcommittee structure to allow the subcommittees to work more effectively with the Forum's action committees. And though most of the people we talked with agree that the process has already paid important dividends in new leadership, neighborhood projects, and a new spirit of optimism in the citizens of Phoenix, they also agree that the real measure of the Forum's success will come well into the future.

The Baltimore Commonwealth

Baltimore is a city of contrasts. In the downtown area, there are glittering waterfront buildings and tourist attractions. Within walking distance of those are run-down and burned-out buildings of an urban slum. Baltimore's demographics are changing. People of color now make up more than 50 percent of the 780,000 population, many of them living well below the poverty line. Illiteracy and school dropout rates hover between 50 and 60 percent. The rate of unmarried births is one of the nation's highest, and the city's AIDS epidemic is one of the nation's worst. Baltimore's economy is in decline. As the traditional core of manufacturing employment shifts to services and technology, there is a growing mismatch between employment needs and the educational level of the work force. The more prosperous residents are fleeing the urban setting for more hospitable suburbs.

In 1984 BUILD (Baltimoreans United in Leadership Development), a grass-roots community-organizing group, set its agenda around three areas: unemployment, housing, and education. The three issues were inseparable, BUILD felt, in terms of their causes and effects. In a precedent-setting symbolic move, BUILD approached the Greater Baltimore Committee (GBC), Baltimore's primary business organization, as a potential partner to address these issues. Over a period of a year or so, a partnership developed with GBC's growing recognition that business work-force needs were closely tied to the educational needs of the community. This partnership became the Baltimore Commonwealth. By 1988 the partnership had been expanded to include several government organizations, the mayor's office, and the Baltimore City Public Schools.

The mission of the partnership is to prepare young people to be responsible, contributing citizens. The Commonwealth does this by establishing programs and incentives designed to keep students in school and to graduate them with the capacity to be economically productive and to be good public citizens. The Commonwealth expects to define the educational competencies needed to meet these goals and, in partnership with the school system, implement systemic reforms to the K–12 educational process.

The Newark Collaboration Group

"Newark may be America's most incredible shrinking city, but its ego is growing," wrote Sam Roberts for the *New York Times* (April 8, 1991, p. B1). In an article reporting the tremendous population loss—30 percent between 1970 and 1990—Roberts says signs of pride and renewal are apparent in a city that was deeply torn and scarred by racial riots in the late sixties.

Much of the city's progress can be attributed to the Newark Collaboration Group (NCG), created in 1984 as a result of the relentless efforts of Prudential executive Alex Plinio to bring together key leaders from all the city's sectors—business, government, nonprofit, neighborhood, academic, and religious. At that time, says Plinio, "there was very little trust, very little hope, no vision, and the governing sector on its own could not manage the city effectively. There were just innumerable problems."

The main purpose of NCG was to facilitate collaborative problem solving around Newark's most difficult issues. The group wanted to provide a forum for bringing people together to talk and find common ground and ways to work together on solutions. Their first task—a process they called "issue discernment"—was an attempt to involve a broad base of citizens in determining the key issues confronting Newark. Through task forces and large public meetings, the group produced a future vision for their city and a strategic plan for getting there, entitled "City Life." These actions led to significant improvements in housing, education, and economic development. In 1991 Newark received the National Civic League's coveted All-America City Award for its collaborative revitalization efforts.

Citizens for Denver's Future

In the late 1980s in Denver, Colorado, Mayor Federico Peña confronted an extremely serious problem with the city's deteriorating physical infrastructure. The city and state were in a deep economic downturn, city leaders had to fight tax limitation measures every two years, and the mayor's popularity was low. The task of developing and winning voter passage of a large bond issue that would increase property taxes seemed nearly impossible. After watching the city of Phoenix use community-wide collaboration to put together a successful bond package for infrastructure funding, the Peña administration decided to try something similar. Peña had a history of using broad-based citizen involvement to solve city problems and had a fair number of people around him and in the community who were experienced with community collaboration.

Peña and the Denver city council put together a ninety-two-person committee—Citizens for Denver's Future—which included representatives of all segments of the city, including business, neighborhoods, government, nonprofit organizations, Democrats, and Republicans. The large committee was divided into smaller working groups that worked with city experts to assess a variety of infrastructure needs (parks, bridges, and so on). The real test of the citizen effort came when the committee found that the city needed over $800 million in infrastructure repair. They agreed that voters would not support a bond issue of that size and decided that somehow they would have to get the total package closer to $200 million.

The task of cutting and prioritizing city projects to be included in the package could have been a disastrous battle of special interests. But the tone and mission of the committee were set and reset along the way by the two committee co-chairs: Tim Sandos, a young Democrat who was a neighborhood activist and grocery store manager, and Harry Lewis, an older Republican who was a corporate executive. They asked committee members not to fight for their own narrow interests. Decisions had to be made in the much broader context of what was best for the community as a whole.

The eighteen-month project was covered heavily by the news media, due to the importance of the issue and the openness of the process. Even though the large citizen committee was very representative of the community, the committee still sought input from the public at large. Forums were held all over the city by the working groups, both in the early phase of determining city infrastructure needs and in the later phase of explaining the final package to voters.

Citizens for Denver's Future came up with a package of ten bond issues totaling over $200 million. The mayor and city council approved the package as a ballot initiative that would increase taxes for each Denver property owner by about $40 a year. The ten bond issues appeared separately on the November 1988 ballot, enabling citizens to vote in favor of some and against others. The political campaign to advocate passage confronted virtually no opposition, and all ten issues passed.

Roanoke Vision

In 1964 Roanoke, Virginia, city planners went behind closed doors and created a comprehensive plan that was destined to wreak havoc on city development for the next twenty years. The plan led to zoning changes (similar to those in other parts of the country) aimed at "urban renewal." The regulations were based on the belief that deteriorating downtown and inner-city areas were best cleaned up by tearing down old structures and building new ones. As a result, Roanoke's downtown and older neighborhoods lost magnificent old buildings to a hodgepodge of commercial, industrial, and multifamily structures.

It was not until the late 1970s that city leaders began to real-ize the failure of their "urban renewal" to affect serious problems—a deteriorating downtown, critical housing problems, housing demolitions, crime, and disinvestment throughout the older areas of the city.

Two collaborative efforts were begun to spark revitalization in Roanoke in 1979. One planning project, Design '79, focused on downtown, while another, the Roanoke Neighborhood Partner-ship, was created to reinvigorate the city's neighborhoods. Both projects used television programs and newspaper surveys to solicit citizen input and interactive workshops to encourage citizen par-ticipation. Later, a third citizen planning effort was undertaken to protect and improve the city's parks.

The business group that produced Design '79 disbanded when the project was completed, but the plan the group created is still lauded today as a collaborative effort of the business sector that indeed revitalized the downtown. The Roanoke Neighborhood Partnership continues today, with half the city's neighborhoods organized and participating. The parks plan has been key to pre-serving another important community asset.

By the mid 1980s, development activities that had been initi-ated by the downtown and neighborhood plans were frequently running into the antiquated 1964 regulatory roadblocks; yet those same 1964 ordinances failed to protect older buildings and areas that the downtown and neighborhood projects were trying to build their revitalization efforts upon.

Earl Reynolds, director of planning in the mid eighties, had been deeply involved in the three earlier collaborative projects, which had been spearheaded by the city manager. Reynolds con-vinced the city manager, Byrne Ewert, that his prized projects would never reach their potential if city policies and regulations were not revamped. It was also clear to these administrators that, while the citizen participation projects had momentum and current administration support, a "changing of the guard" could sud-denly bring an end to their efforts.

A new comprehensive plan (to replace the one on which the 1964 regulations were based)—this one citizen-supported—would bind the city to the values, vision, and direction expressed in the recent collaborative projects. Most important, it would facilitate implementation of strategies advocated in the neighborhood, busi-ness, and parks plans by asserting the need for new city policies and zoning regulations.

A comprehensive-plan citizen advisory committee and an ordi-nance review committee were appointed by the city council to help guide the process and make recommendations. A special insert appeared in the local newspaper asserting the importance of com-munity planning, describing the Roanoke Vision process, and ask-ing for citizens to respond by returning an enclosed questionnaire. A local commercial television station ran a special program describ-ing the project and issues involved. It included a call-in segment during which people could voice their concerns about the direc-tion of city development. A large Roanoke Vision Forum was held, in town meeting style, that brought together 200 civic, business, neighborhood, and government leaders. Through a series of three planning workshops, a list of values and specific concerns was for-mulated by citizens to guide the development of the comprehen-sive plan. In addition, the city planning staff attended meetings of a large number of community organizations to discuss the project and solicit concerns and ideas.

With this information, the city staff and consultants produced the plan. At its heart is a section on values and recommendations designed to guide development. What seems to be most significant in this section is the following: protection of neighborhoods, con-tinued economic development without neighborhood damage, and preservation of important historical assets.

To a significant degree, it appears that the comprehensive plan has had the impact that was intended. Newspaper reporter Joel Turner says that both the administration and citizen groups cite it when making a case for or against certain city actions. It (along with accompanying zoning changes) has facilitated downtown and neighborhood development.

American Leadership Forum

Our search for exemplary cases led us to a unique organization, the American Leadership Forum (ALF). We were familiar with ALF through our previous research on successful teams and through the leadership training and consulting that we had done with the organization. It had been frequently and favorably cited for the collaborative projects that had been sparked by its leadership development program. Rather than responding to specific problems, as the other exemplary cases did, ALF created networks of leaders in several different communities who then took on difficult issues in collaborative ways. ALF so clearly embodied collaborative principles that we added it to our sample of exemplary cases.

The American Leadership Forum was founded in 1980 by Joe Jaworski, a successful Houston trial attorney. Jaworski describes his personal response to the oft-lamented leadership crisis of the 1970s as follows:

Perspectives began changing in the '70s. People around age 40 were basically discouraged from stepping out and leading the community, region, or nation. As a result, a sort of civic cynicism was growing up.

I began feeling all of those things in the mid-70s. Watergate had just finished, and my dad [Leon Jaworski] had been deeply involved, and it touched me deeply as well. I had rightly or wrongly understood that "they" were in charge out there in Washington, or elsewhere, and everything was okay. All we had to do was our little piece of it. This was obviously totally wrong, and the Watergate experience pulled me up sharply and made me really begin thinking about how we each need to contribute, or we are in real trouble.

I went off to London for three years because I had committed to building our firm's office there. When you move away from it all, you see things more clearly.

I really put this whole leadership issue together in my mind about 1975. By 1980, everybody was writing about it, and I had this plan for American Leadership Forum. I felt like the timing was right—Russians had marched on Afghanistan; Carter had the Iranian crisis; economic problems were generating massive social problems. *Time* magazine did a special issue on the leadership gap, as did *Newsweek* and *U.S. News & World Report*. I felt a personal need to try and do something.

The ultimate vision was to put in each community a smaller community of strengthened leaders who had shared perspectives about making that place a better place to live—people who would literally begin taking responsibility for what happened in that community [Larson and LaFasto, 1989, p. 44].

The first American Leadership Forum program was completed in Houston in 1983. Though the goals have been refined over time, the original principles envisioned by Jaworski continue to govern the design and delivery of the program. First, ALF identifies and brings together leaders from different sectors of the community and prepares them to work together on significant issues. Second, ALF heightens the leaders' sense of public responsibility and their commitment to act upon that responsibility. Third, ALF builds the collaborative skills and competencies required to meet leadership challenges.

In pursuit of these goals, the ALF program brings together from twenty to twenty-four of a community's leaders, including corporate executives, public officials, and leaders in education, labor, religion, art, media, and the professions. These individuals make up a class. The class is administered and supported by a local chapter. Presently, yearly classes are convened in Houston (since 1983), Hartford (since 1985), Portland, serving the state of Oregon (since 1987), Tacoma (since 1989), and San Jose, serving Silicon Valley (since 1989).

Each class experiences a program of approximately twenty days' duration over a year. The program is predominantly experiential, notably in its "wilderness challenge"—a six-day Outward Bound experience emphasizing risk taking and vision, collaborative problem solving, trust, and teamwork—and in the "leadership in action" segment, in which participants "learn by doing" a project of value to the community.

ALF members address community issues in collaborative efforts growing out of the informal ALF network and in organized "class projects" completed at the end of each group's year-long leadership training program. As one example of the sort of project resulting from ALF's program for strengthening leadership and collaboration, Houston ALF Fellows helped make prenatal, maternity, and support services available to all indigent pregnant women in the Houston metropolitan area. Let us look at that example in some detail.

While many agencies and organizations were concerned with the problems confronting indigent pregnant women, most worked at cross-purposes. Nearly one-third of all indigent pregnant women received late or no prenatal care, the infant mortality rate exceeded state and national averages, and almost 20 percent of the babies had low birth weights.

Spurred by the interest of one Fellow concerned with educating teenage mothers about good prenatal care, ALF acted as a convening and focusing force for thirty-five social agencies. ALF brought all the interested agencies and organizations together, and its Fellows served as facilitators in planning and managing the collaborative process. Over the course of a year, a series of meetings led to the planning and implementation of specific projects that would eliminate redundant spending and unify efforts toward one goal.

The coalition began with a needs assessment that identified four major problem areas. Patients were facing an incomprehensible bureaucracy due in part to the lack of communication and coordination among providers. Additionally, public prenatal care did not address the more comprehensive health needs of the patient, and social support and outreach programs were not available. In response, the coalition created a computer network, now installed in all county and city clinics, that gives each provider access to full medical records. They set up a single screening program for patient qualification (where four or six visits were previously required), and they established a program to reduce infant mortality and morbidity. By eliminating competition for funds, they developed services that addressed patient needs and lowered costs to both patients and providers.

The Keys to Successful Collaboration

Our study of these six exemplary cases helped us establish some preliminary conclusions about what makes collaboration succeed. We tested these conclusions against forty-six additional cases, again selected with the help of the National Civic League. (See Appendix A.) Some of our preliminary conclusions were confirmed; others were not. Those that were confirmed are the factors that, depending upon their presence or absence, determine whether collaboration will succeed or fail. These are the things that must be present or deliberately built into the process from the beginning in order for collaboration to succeed:

• *Good timing and clear need.* The initiation of the project was timely in that some stakeholders were ready to act in response to a clear need. There was a sense of urgency that provided initial momentum to the effort.

• *Strong stakeholder groups.* The city or region had strong stakeholder groups that represented many people and/or organizations. These groups were well organized and could speak and act credibly for the interests they represented. (For example, a strong chamber of commerce may broadly represent the business community; an association of neighborhood organizations may be able to speak credibly for its members.)

• *Broad-based involvement.* The effort involved many participants from several sectors—for example, government, business, and community groups—as opposed to few participants predominantly from one sector.

• *Credibility and openness of process.* The process was seen as credible by the participating stakeholders: it was considered fair and was not seen as dominated by any particular stakeholder group. In addition, the effort was seen as doing meaningful work rather than simply rubber stamping; stakeholders participated in decision making or in providing input that influenced decisions. The process was open in that stakeholders were free to participate as they felt necessary; important stakeholders were not purposefully excluded from the process. Norms or ground rules for participation and meeting behavior were established (explicitly or implicitly) that supported the credibility and openness of the process. The commitment of the participants was, at least in part, secured by the credibility and openness of the process.

- *Commitment and/or involvement of high-level, visible leaders.* The effort was characterized by the commitment and/or involvement of high-level, visible leaders such as mayors, city council members, chief executive officers, and executive directors. When these leaders were not directly involved, their commitment to the process was still obvious. When they were represented by other parties, they delegated decision-making power to the representatives. Their support brought credibility to the effort and was an essential aspect of the success of the endeavor.

- *Support or acquiescence of "established" authorities or powers.* "Established" authorities or powers, such as city councils, mayors, and chambers of commerce, agreed to support and abide by the recommendations of the stakeholder groups arrived at through the collaborative process. They did not undermine the results of the project by refusing to live with the recommendations. Their ability to provide support came, in part, because they or their constituencies were effectively represented in the process.

- *Overcoming mistrust and skepticism.* In the early phases of the project (perhaps when the participants were first learning about the idea behind the project or when the initial meetings were being planned or held), some or many participants were generally skeptical about whether anything significant would be accomplished. In some cases, there was some mistrust about the motives or objectives of those who had initiated the project; in other cases, there was a history of mistrust between different sectors or stakeholders. This skepticism or mistrust decreased over time.

- *Strong leadership of the process.* The effort was characterized by at least a few (often many) examples of strong leadership of the process rather than strong leadership through advocacy of a particular point of view. Leadership of the process was exhibited in many ways: among them, keeping stakeholders at the table through periods of frustration and skepticism, acknowledging small successes along the way, helping stakeholders negotiate difficult points, and enforcing group norms and ground rules.

- *Interim successes.* The effort was characterized by interim successes along the way. These successes built and sustained credibility and momentum. They provided encouragement that something was really happening and helped secure the commitment of the stakeholders to the process. These successes were acknowledged and celebrated.

- *A shift to broader concerns.* As the effort evolved, the participants focused less on narrow, parochial interests and more on the broader interests of the community. They seemed to recognize that their ability to do something about complex issues required them to collaborate as equal partners rather than as advocates of particular interests.

These "lessons of experience" from our research form the basis of the remainder of the book. In the following four chapters we will expand on each of these lessons and share with you, in the words of the participants, what makes collaboration work and what leadership practices are necessary to sustain it.

Chapter Four

Setting the Stage for Success

Niccolò Machiavelli is notorious for his advocacy of "Machiavellian" practices of leadership. In his early-sixteenth-century book *The Prince*, he recommends that leaders do whatever is necessary to achieve their ends and to maintain themselves in power. His blunt recommendations still shock readers. For instance, he asserts, "Hence it is necessary to a prince, if he wants to maintain himself, to learn to be able not to be good, and to use this and not use it according to necessity" ([1532] 1985, p. 61). For Machiavelli, the objective of the leader is to win at any cost. He wants leaders to recognize that power is finite: if you want power, you must take it from someone else. He observes that self-interest or fear motivates most people and that leaders can use these motivations to manipulate others to act on their behalf. Above all, he wants leaders to be pragmatic: they should use those leadership practices that will work to achieve their ends. These recommendations are Machiavelli's most famous (or infamous) legacy. But he leaves other, more important lessons that few people recognize.

For example, Machiavelli knows that leaders must carefully analyze and understand the context for leadership before acting. He knows that leaders must understand the motivations of both followers and leaders. He knows that leaders must have a range of leadership practices in their repertoire and must choose those practices that are most likely to achieve results in a particular situation. He is concerned to know what leadership strategies will work to achieve desired ends. While we may abhor many of the leadership practices Machiavelli advocates, citizens and civic leaders alike would do well to heed his practice of understanding the context before choosing a leadership strategy for creating change. Successful collaborative initiatives depend on a thorough understanding of the motivation and the context for working together.

Understanding the Motivation to Collaborate

Collaborative initiatives are responses to real needs. Sometimes these needs are concrete, visible, and compelling. When Mayor Federico Peña initiated Citizens for Denver's Future (CDF) in 1988, the city's physical infrastructure was in frightful condition. Viaducts crossing the central Platte Valley were crumbling. According to Penelope Purdy, a *Denver Post* reporter who looked at the bridges, "Bridges are rated on a scale of 0 to 100 (100 is best) on a number of criteria—their ability to carry traffic, ease of entry and access, lighting, and safety. 20th Street bridge is a 6." Lanes were closed on some bridges to prevent overloading. Others were shored up to prevent collapse. Drivers dodged potholes in uneven streets. Older trees around parks were dying and not being replaced. Recreation centers were deteriorating. Lee White, an investment banker and member of the CDF task force, notes that the physical infrastructure bond initiative was not simply foisted on a community suffering from too much public works: "There were root problems to be solved."

Timing, too, was important. Peña wanted to do something quickly about the city's physical infrastructure. He also knew that in order to carry a large bond initiative in the midst of a serious recession and a rising tide of "no new taxes" sentiment, he would need to bring together a group of citizens representing all parts of Denver to define the infrastructure needs and priorities. He wanted the group to develop a consensus that would be approved both by the city council and by the voters in the upcoming bond election. By this time, it was easy to convince citizens to work together; the needs were clear and the timing was right.

In Baltimore, though, it took more than a clear need and good timing to get people to collaborate. In the early 1980s, many of Baltimore's citizens recognized the serious problems in the city's schools. Dropout rates were high, and few graduates of local high schools were prepared to work in business, to raise families, or to be good citizens. Teen pregnancies and drug use were skyrocketing. The number of minority students going on to college was extraordinarily low. Despite these obvious failures, the school system—Baltimore City Public Schools (BCPS)—took little initiative to address the problems. Instead, a grass-roots organization, Baltimoreans United in Leadership Development (BUILD), provided the spark that eventually led to the formation of the Baltimore Commonwealth, a partnership of business and community organizations, city government, and BCPS.

The BUILD organization was a product of the Industrial Areas Foundation (IAF), which was started by Saul Alinsky, the radical grass-roots organizer of the 1950s and 1960s. Arnie Graf, IAF's lead organizer in Baltimore, helped get BUILD started in the early 1980s. Graf and others successfully organized a large part of the African-American community, establishing BUILD as a strong and effective advocate for the poor. The organization reflected its radical roots with its confrontational strategies to gain power from other groups in the city. These tactics isolated BUILD from other parts of the city. BUILD's stances on bank redlining and utility rate increases especially strained relationships with the Greater Baltimore Committee (GBC), the organization representing the city's business interests.

By 1984 BUILD's primary goals were to improve education, build low-income housing, and create employment opportunities for African-Americans. A few members of the organization began to see the linkages between these issues, and they recognized that GBC might share some of their concerns. BUILD's leaders knew that GBC was the central power in Baltimore along with elected leaders at a second level. If BUILD was to achieve its agenda, GBC would have to be dealt with. Rather than seeing the power and organization of GBC as a threat, BUILD saw GBC's strength as an opportunity. Graf remembers, "We saw it as an opportunity because we knew that we had somebody to negotiate with." BUILD's strategy was to get enough power to get GBC into a negotiating stance.

BUILD's strengths also presented an opportunity to GBC, whose members began to see the possibilities of working with an organization with a large constituency in the black community. In the past, they had found themselves working with one black elected official while being called racist by another. Now they had a chance to work with the African-American community on problems that could help businesses satisfy their needs for qualified employees by improving education. Together the two organizations—two strong stakeholder groups—might have enough power to bring the city government and BCPS into a workable partnership to improve education.

The unlikely partnership between a radical black community organization and the white pillars of the establishment took some getting used to. Several BUILD members accused the lead organizers of selling out to the business community. Meanwhile, business leaders were afraid that BUILD would resume its confrontational tactics if things did not go its way. BUILD was at risk because it had made an agreement with a historical enemy; GBC was at risk because it was not clear that it could gain the black community's trust. An uncharacteristic act of leadership cemented the partnership: Bob Keller, GBC's president, went to speak before 1,500 people at Big Valley Baptist Church in the black community. The event, says Keller, built on the formal agreement between BUILD and GBC that was signed just before the meeting. "What happened out of this," he explains, "was that the contract became covenant. We really began to understand that we share values and that there was a larger issue of trust and that the real issue was sharing power." The combined influence of two powerful stakeholder groups in the community eventually brought the city government and the school system into the partnership. Now, says Keller, "BUILD and GBC are recognized publicly and formally as an alliance and a pressure group around the schools, and that is taken seriously by the community." Despite widespread recognition among Baltimore residents of problems in the schools, sufficient momentum had to be created to force the reluctant parties, especially the school system, into addressing the problems collaboratively. None of the parties could do it alone, and nothing else was working.

An essential task of leaders who know that they must collaborate is to understand, as BUILD's and GBC's leaders did, what it takes to get people to work together and then figure out how to get them to the table. In Denver, Mayor Peña took advantage of a time when the city's infrastructure needs were most visible to convene concerned citizens; in Baltimore, BUILD's leaders brought together two strong, well-organized stakeholder groups with complementary objectives, and these groups used their combined power and influence to motivate others to collaborate.

Understanding the Context of Collaboration

In Chapter One, we suggested that success in collaboration depends upon our ability to bring the appropriate people together in constructive ways with good information to achieve results. As a preliminary step, then, we have to understand the context for leadership in order to identify the appropriate people, design constructive processes, and provide good information. There are several aspects of this initial leadership task:

- Identify the problem type.
- Understand what makes leadership difficult.
- Identify the relevant community of interests: the stakeholders.
- Assess the extent of stakeholder agreement.
- Evaluate the community's capacity for change.
- Identify where the problem/issue can be most effectively addressed.

Identify the Problem Type

U.S. communities define themselves, in part, by the challenges they face. Each place proclaims its character by the uniqueness of its problems. Hartford, Connecticut, Tampa, Florida, and Cleveland, Ohio, seem as different as the cultures they represent. The problems they list—pollution and poverty, environment and education, crime and drugs, transportation and health care, growth or decline—are peculiar, they argue, to their circumstances. Yet under the outward differences, there are striking similarities in the political dynamics of the issues.

Many people—individual citizens and innumerable interest groups—are affected by and involved in the issues. No one person or group can solve the problem alone. There are no "experts" who can "fix" the problem for the stakeholders. Responsibility and jurisdiction are murky. The issues are messy and inseparable from others. For example, a policy affecting transportation will have consequences, often unforeseen, for air quality. Different interests bring many solutions to the table, yet there is little agreement on the nature of the problem. For instance, do easily purchased guns cause violent crimes, or are there other, less visible causes? Many of the challenges—air pollution, for example—require changes in behavior by people. Thus technological or capital-intensive responses are not enough in themselves to adequately deal with some issues. And there are no big, "once and forever" fixes.

One way of comprehending these dynamics is through a typology of problems. Ronald Heifetz and Riley Sinder propose such a typology using a medical analogy (Heifetz and Sinder, 1988). Some problems are readily definable and have known solutions; they are routine challenges. All we need to do is find the expert who knows how to fix them. For example, a broken leg is easily diagnosed and treated by an orthopedic doctor. Heifetz and Sinder call these Type I problems.

A second category, Type II, encompasses problems that are clearly defined but whose solution requires action and thought on the part of those affected. This sort of problem cannot be fixed solely by the expert. A patient with heart problems, for example, can be treated to some extent by surgery and medication, but longer-term health is dependent on the patient's active involvement. He or she may have to change life style, diet, and exercise patterns. The doctor or the expert can diagnose the problem but cannot "fix" it. Some pollution problems in the public policy arena are Type II problems. The sources of the pollution are known, but there is little agreement about who is responsible or about what solutions are appropriate. Many people may have to change behaviors or take specific actions to implement a solution. Getting their agreement is difficult.

Sometimes neither the problem nor the solution is definable by the physician or expert—a Type III problem. For example, a doctor may diagnose a patient's condition as a form of cancer that is likely to be terminal and for which there is no known cure. From there, the problem must be defined by the patient, not the doctor. For example, the patient may see the problem as how to get the most out of life, how to deal with relatives, or any number of other dilemmas. The solutions, too, are up to the patient. In communities, drug problems are of the Type III variety. Everyone knows something is wrong, but there is little agreement about whether it is a supply problem or a demand problem. How we define the problem will determine whether the solution is a "war on drugs" or a campaign to "just say no" to drug use. With no agreement about the definition of the problem, there can be no agreement about solutions. Table 4.1 is adapted from Heifetz and Sinder's work to fit public policy situations.

Most challenges faced by this country's communities and regions are of the Type II or Type III variety. We know little about working with these kinds of issues, however, because they demand

Table 4.1. Problem Types.

	Problem Definition	Solution	Primary Locus of Work
Type I	Clear	Clear	Leader
Type II	Clear	Unclear	Leader/Constituents
Type III	Unclear	Unclear	Constituents

Source: Adapted from Heifetz and Sinder, 1988, p. 186.

the involvement of many constituents or stakeholders in defining the problems and in creating and implementing solutions. The problems are too big for one group to solve alone. Successfully addressing Type II and Type III problems is a heuristic political and social learning process. These problems are adaptive, not routine, challenges; there are no experts. They pose new challenges for both leaders and followers. In Heifetz and Sinder's words, the primary objective of public leadership is "turning the work of the community back over to the community" (p. 201).

Before beginning a collaborative initiative, citizens and civic leaders need to know the type of problem or issue they face. Is it a Type I, Type II, or Type III problem? In Denver the physical infrastructure issue was a Type II problem. The Infrastructure Group, made up of administration and city council members, completed a thorough analysis of the city's needs in 1987. The report showed Denver needing more than $800 million of repairs and improvements. But a public opinion poll indicated that a bond package exceeding $300 million would be unlikely to pass at election time. The problem was clear: how to prioritize the city's needs to fit within the financing capacity. Peña knew that establishing these priorities would require more than the strength of city hall. This work had to be done by members of the community in order to ensure passage of the bond package.

Newark faced a different situation: the city had many Type III problems. Most people in the city knew that something was drastically wrong and that the problems were overwhelming, but no one knew where to start. Neither problems nor solutions were clear. The problems and issues had to be defined by a "relevant community of interests" before the city could progress to solutions. No person or group had enough power to move ahead unilaterally.

By identifying the problem type, leaders can quickly determine whether they can do the problem-solving work themselves or whether their task is to create a constituency for change by convening and catalyzing the relevant people to do the work.

Understand What Makes Leadership Difficult

In many places, we have asked the question, "What makes leadership difficult on the issues your city faces?" The answers are similar whether the issue is education, health care, injustice, economic development, or something else equally challenging. Take your pick: There are many people with the power to say no, yet no one person or group has the power to act alone. People do not trust each other. There are hidden agendas. There is no larger vision that brings coherence to actions. No person or group has enough credibility to provide leadership. Nobody will take a leadership role. People lack the leadership capacities or group skills to work together constructively. There are not enough resources to address the problem. Most citizens are apathetic; they will not take responsibility for shared problems. Leaders and citizens avoid risk for fear of being attacked by others. The problems are complex and interdependent; they cross jurisdictional boundaries. No one is in charge. Many people do not know what the "real" problem is. Information about problems distorts understanding. And so on.

Most of these observations reflect the inability of people to work together constructively. They have little to do with the substance of the issues or problems. This is an important distinction:

it means the primary focus of leadership when people have to collaborate needs to be on the "process" of how people work together to solve problems, not on the "content" of the problem itself. If the relevant community of interests is brought together in constructive ways (process) with good information, they will come up with appropriate responses (content).

All of the answers to the question, "What makes leadership difficult?" provide useful information for leaders. Each answer indicates an obstacle that must be dealt with and suggests how a constructive process needs to be designed. If people do not know how to work together, for example, teach them. (In Newark, Prudential vice president Alex Plinio hired David Straus of Interaction Associates to help the Newark Collaboration Group [NCG] learn to work together.) If there is no agreement about the vision for the city or region, create an initiative whereby citizens can explore and agree on future needs and direction. (The Phoenix Futures Forum and Roanoke Vision projects defined a desired future that provided a context for decision and action.) If no one has the power to act unilaterally or if no one is in charge, build a collaborative partnership (like the Baltimore Commonwealth) that brings together several strong stakeholder groups that can act collectively on issues of shared concern. If no one person or group has the strength or credibility to provide leadership, develop a structure for sharing leadership. (Citizens for Denver's Future was co-chaired by a retired Republican investment banker—one of the city's "established" leaders—and a young Democratic, Hispanic community activist.) When collaborative initiatives work, leadership challenges are consciously addressed.

Identify the Relevant Community of Interests: The Stakeholders

The term *stakeholder* originally meant a person entrusted with the stakes of bettors. Later meanings were derived from marking out land claims with wooden stakes—the claimant becoming the stakeholder. More recent usage defines a stakeholder as one who is affected by or affects a particular problem or issue. In the context of collaboration, the term means those people who are responsible for problems or issues, those who are affected by them, those whose perspectives or knowledge are needed to develop good solutions or strategies, and those who have the power and resources to block or implement solutions and strategies. It is the stakeholders in collaborative initiatives who need to do the work of defining problems and solutions, because it is their work, not the work of a small, exclusive group of leaders, that will lead to action. The stakeholders are those people who, if they were to reach agreement, could act together to achieve real results. Thus identifying stakeholders is the first step in creating a constituency for change. Once this is accomplished, leaders can create strategies to bring those stakeholders into a collaborative process or otherwise gain their acceptance (or overcome their influence). There are several questions that must be answered in the stakeholder identification process:

- What are the perspectives necessary to credibly and effectively define problems/issues and create solutions?
- Who are the people who can speak for these perspectives?
- What are the interests that must be represented in order to reach agreements that can be implemented?
- Who are the people who can speak for these interests?
- Who are the people, interest groups, or organizations who are necessary to implement solutions, can block action, and control resources?
- Who are the people who cause or are affected by the problems/issues, and who will be affected by the solutions?
- Who are the people who, if they could reach agreement about problems and solutions, could generate the political and institutional will to create significant change?

Identifying stakeholders begins with an analysis of the perspectives necessary for defining problems and solutions, not with the names of powerful individuals or organizations that need to be represented. The perspectives of those affected by problems or solutions and those who may be part of the cause of problems are especially important. Understanding perspectives also provides an opportunity to draw new people into civic endeavors rather than rely on the usual "suspects" who most often participate. When Roanoke began to address its dying downtown and deteriorating neighborhoods, organizers brought in "ordinary" citizens to help. Among them was Barbara Duerk, who thought no one would listen to what she had to say, "being just a housewife and not really having any power behind me." But when those running the Roanoke Vision process responded to the ideas of citizens, she changed her belief: "My opinion *does* count." The city's director of planning, Earl Reynolds, says, "We knew that the only way we were going to make any kind of a significant change was to involve the persons that were going to be affected by the change and get them to buy in."

Differing perspectives enhance the wisdom brought to problem-solving efforts and the possibilities for real change. Expanding the pool of stakeholders can help overcome some of the obstacles that make leadership difficult by creating a broader power base. Opening up the definition of stakeholders is a crucial step in creating a constituency for change that goes beyond the traditional terms of money, power, and position.

Once perspectives have been defined, traditional power players, interest groups, and organizations can be identified. When BUILD members began to think about their agenda for education and jobs, they recognized early on the importance of the business community (GBC) as a key stakeholder, along with the schools (BCPS) and city government. BUILD used its common interest with the business community—high school graduates who could participate successfully in the work force—to establish a strong partnership with GBC. Without this relationship, members of BUILD would not have had enough influence or power to induce the schools to work with them. By understanding the interests of the stakeholders who are necessary to implement solutions, those who can block action, and those who control power and resources, leaders can create strategies to either bring them in to a collaborative endeavor or overcome their resistance.

Assess the Extent of Stakeholder Agreement

When people finally decide to work together, they usually begin by arguing for the different solutions they bring to the table. This "war of solutions" leads nowhere, because it is the wrong place to start. Stakeholders need to reach other, preliminary agreements before they can begin to discuss problems and agree on solutions. By asking a series of questions about the status and extent of stakeholder agreement, leaders will know where to begin in designing a collaborative initiative. Here are six questions to help assess the extent of stakeholder agreement:

- Have stakeholders agreed there is a problem that needs attention?
- Have stakeholders agreed to work together on the problem/issue?
- Have stakeholders agreed on *how* to work together on the problem/issue?
- Have stakeholders agreed on the definition of the problem/issue?
- Have stakeholders agreed on the solution(s) to the problem/issue?
- Have stakeholders agreed on an implementation plan and action steps?

In the mid 1980s, Phoenix was riding the crest of a thirty-year growth wave that had fueled the local economy. One observer described Phoenix as "a city whose biggest business was itself." The perennially strong economy created an air of complacency, allowing leaders and citizens to overlook serious problems caused by the rapid growth. For one thing, the city's capacity to plan for and deliver services had failed to keep pace with expanding needs. Schools and human service agencies struggled to meet the needs of the growing population. Regional problems such as air quality, hazardous waste disposal, and transportation were becoming increasingly difficult to deal with because they went beyond jurisdictional lines. Despite these problems, optimistic reports and forecasts about Phoenix's future continued to be written. Two Arizona State University professors describe the city's optimism at that time as "collective self-deception and selective denial" (Hall and Weschler, 1991, p. 140). The immediate challenge for Phoenix was to generate widespread agreement among citizens that problems existed in order to create enough impetus to address them.

In Newark, no one needed to be convinced that the city faced monumental problems. For years, various people and groups had attempted, with great frustration, to deal with the problems—but always in piecemeal ways. It was not clear that anyone had the energy to address the problems in a more comprehensive and systematic fashion. With general agreement about Newark's problems, something had to be done to find out if the city's residents cared enough to work together.

The stakeholders in any community rarely have agreement beyond that of shared recognition of problems or of the need to work together. Because any process for working together must start where the stakeholders are, not where we imagine or want them to be, the next step in the process is developing a strategy to take stakeholders to subsequent levels of agreement.

Evaluate the Community's Capacity for Change

Another aspect of the context that needs to be evaluated is the capacity of a community's leaders and citizens to bring about change. If working relationships and the capacities and skills to work together do not exist in the leadership and broader community, they must be developed. The following questions help assess a community's capacity for change:

- What is the level of conflict, mistrust, and disunity that exists among the stakeholders?
- To what extent do the skills necessary for collaboration exist in the community?
- Are there leaders with the credibility and respect to convene stakeholders around the problems or issues? Who are they?
- Are there citizens with the leadership capacities to initiate and sustain a collaborative process? Who are they?
- Are there people or groups in the community with the expertise to design and facilitate a collaborative process?
- Are there people or groups who can provide the information necessary to make good decisions? Who are they? If they do not exist within the community, what are other sources for this information?

Alex Plinio and others recognized that the way Newark's leaders usually solved problems—interest-based political dealing on narrowly defined issues—would not work on the complex, interconnected, and deep-seated concerns Newark now faced. They decided, instead, to work by consensus. Only in this way could every stakeholder have a say and be a part of the decision-making process. But the capacity of stakeholders to work by consensus did not yet exist in Newark. As a result of Plinio's research into what was working in other cities, he concluded that he needed to bring in "process" experts to build trust among stakeholders, guide the first meetings, and help teach consensus-building skills to participants. He knew that without enhancing the ability of the city's leaders to collaborate, NCG would likely fail. Learning to work together would have to be part of the process design.

Other communities have used different means to build their civic capacity to create change. In Hartford, Connecticut, Denis Mullane, chairman of Connecticut Mutual Life Insurance, remembers the early 1980s—the period just after the city's corporate leaders, the "bishops," had lost influence. "The old order was no longer in place, and no new order was there in terms of community leadership." Affluent whites were fleeing to the suburbs. Black and Hispanic neighborhood groups were becoming stronger. There was little communication among the different parts of the city. When people from the various enclaves did talk, it was confrontational. Mullane says, "Obviously there was significant mistrust and lots of misconceptions about how bad the other guys were." Hartford had no leaders with the credibility or the capacity to bring the different parts of the community together in useful ways.

Rather than waiting for a particular issue or problem to force people to develop their capacity to collaborate, Mullane and other Hartford leaders took a more proactive, long-term approach. They decided to start a revolutionary leadership development program. Using a leadership development model created by the American Leadership Forum (ALF), they established the Hartford Chapter of ALF in 1984. The program developed by this chapter was designed to identify and bring together leaders, build working relationships of trust and respect, heighten participants' sense of public responsibility, and enhance their leadership skills and competencies to meet Hartford's challenges. Over the years, a cadre of leaders from all parts of the community would be developed who could work together. Mullane believed that "this might be a forum through which a different kind of leadership would emerge." And that belief looks to be well founded: as the number of citizens who have been a part of the ALF program has grown, Hartford's readiness and capacity for change have been significantly enhanced. Many of the participants have sparked collaborative projects to address specific problems and are regarded by those who know them as important assets in the city's civic infrastructure.

Identify Where the Issue Can Be Most Effectively Addressed

If issues are complex and responsibility and accountability are murky, it is important to determine whether problems can be most effectively addressed at the neighborhood, community, city, regional, or state level.

When the Montana Water Quality Bureau held a public hearing in 1983 on Champion International's request to dump its pulp mill waste into the Clark Fork River, many people from Idaho showed up. The plant manager had expected opposition from Missoula residents and environmental groups but not from a neighboring state. A coalition of environmentalists and citizens eventually negotiated a solution to Champion's waste problems without damaging the river. This led, in 1988, to the beginning of the State of the Clark Fork Project, which began to redefine jurisdiction for the Clark Fork River based on the geographic extent of its watershed. This included the river basin and tributaries in Montana and Idaho. The mayor of Missoula, Daniel Kemmis— one of the project's founders—says that the project was a way to get inhabitants of the basin to "become more directly, more creatively, and more cooperatively involved in meeting the challenges of the river system." He wanted it to create opportunities for "river basin citizenship" (1989, p. 5). He and others had learned that issues affecting the quality of the Clark Fork watershed could not be resolved in Missoula or even in Montana. The problems were regional, not local.

The question of where most effectively to address change efforts arose in Roanoke, Virginia, too. In the mid 1980s, regulatory road-blocks stymied revitalization efforts in Roanoke's neighborhoods and downtown. Working independently, the downtown planning project (Design '79) and the Roanoke Neighborhood Partnership made little headway against the outdated regulations. The planning manager, Earl Reynolds, knew that the projects developed by these groups could fail unless the city itself revised the regulations. These were issues that could not be handled at the neighborhood or downtown level. The city was responsible for defining a comprehensive plan that would support revitalization at both levels. Based on Reynolds's insight, the Roanoke Vision Forum was formed to advance a new set of guidelines for the city's development. Thus in both Montana and Roanoke, leaders understood where the problems or issues could be most effectively addressed.

Designing a Collaborative Initiative

In February of 1993, *Business Week* published an article entitled "The Virtual Corporation." The authors of that article describe the virtual corporation as "a temporary network of independent companies—suppliers, customers, even erstwhile rivals. . . . It will have no central office nor organization chart. It will have no hierarchy, no vertical integration. Instead, proponents say this new, evolving corporate model will be fluid and flexible—a group of collaborators that quickly unite to exploit a specific opportunity. Once the opportunity is met, the venture will, more often than not, disband" (Byrne, Brandt, and Port, 1993, p. 99). The key attributes of the virtual organization include trust (the fate of each partner is dependent on the action of others), technology (informational networks help companies to link up and work together), excellence (each partner brings its "core competence" to the effort), opportunism (companies band together to meet a specific need and disband once the need evaporates), and open borders (increased cooperation among competitors, suppliers, and customers makes it harder to determine where one company ends and another begins).

Change a few business-oriented words, and these attributes of the virtual corporation could be the attributes of effective collaboration in communities. In successful collaborative initiatives, participants work together as peers; share a collective fate; bring their "core competence" to the table—their perspectives, interests, and experiences; create a sense of community that breaks down barriers (borders) between groups; form networks to work together; and convene around specific needs and then, more often than not, disband when the needs are met. *Collaborative efforts to deal with community issues are "virtual" endeavors.* Each one is different—a unique process created to meet specific needs in a particular situation. There is no "model" collaborative process that will work on all issues in every community. There is no one right answer.

This "virtual" aspect demands a different set of skills from leaders. One of the most important is the capacity to analyze and understand, in a Machiavellian way, the particular context or situation and then to intervene in ways that create and sustain useful change. Leaders have to build agreement about needs, create or take advantage of good timing, develop working relationships among stakeholders, and provide a balance of attention on the process of working together and the need to get results (content). Their primary task is to create a constituency for change that can reach implementable agreements on problems and issues of shared concern, not to impose a specific solution that they themselves have defined. When they accomplish that task—and only then— will real, sustainable results be achieved.

Chapter Five

Creating a Constituency for Change

In order for collaboration to work, certain conditions are so basic that they must be planned for and promoted from the beginning. Achieving useful results requires creating a constituency for change that has the breadth and the integrity to push beyond the parochial interests that prevent people from addressing the broader public concerns of citizens.

The first condition of successful collaboration is that it must be broadly inclusive of all stakeholders (including those who may be "troublesome") who are affected by or care about the issue. And their participation must be not simply tolerated but actively *sought*. It is better to err on the side of too many participants than too few. Second, a credible and open collaborative process must be created so that participants will be confident that their views will be heard and considered and that there are no predetermined outcomes. Participants must know that it is an engagement of peers with no one group or interest in a dominant position. Third, there must be visible support of some high-level, well-known, and trustworthy leaders in the community. This support provides the credibility necessary to assure participants that their efforts may lead to tangible results. Fourth, the support or acquiescence of "established authorities" or institutions who will be needed to implement decisions must be sought at the beginning of the process or gained as a result of the success of the collaborative effort.

The Basic Conditions of Successful Collaboration

When you begin to think about initiating a collaborative process, start with the fundamentals. This is true of any set of complex behaviors, from playing golf to coaching a team to leading an organization. The more complex the behavior, the more important it is to attend to the fundamentals. You must have the fundamentals well in hand in order to succeed. Infinitely more complex than playing golf, coaching a team, or leading an organization is the task of creating and sustaining collaboration, especially when it crosses individual agendas, group identities and loyalties, and organizational and institutional boundaries. Concentrate on the basics. If your attention and efforts are focused on the fundamental principles for initiating a collaborative process, you are more likely to succeed.

Create Broad-Based Involvement

Tim Sandos, co-chair of Citizens for Denver's Future, identifies an important reason for the success of this very difficult collaborative effort: "The idea was to try to include everyone, so that they were part of the decision-making process as it was going, rather than waiting until we had a final package, present to them, and have them chop it up or tear it apart. Everybody had to be involved from the very beginning." Frank Fiore describes the Phoenix Futures Forum in similar terms: "The policy committee did a really good job of selecting people from all different walks of life, all the different social classes, all the different interests. All the extremes were well represented." Another interviewee accounts for his project's success by referring to the "exquisite job done of including just about every cross-section of the community that was possible. Each part of town was represented because council members appointed people from their districts, and then the mayor had a number of at-large appointments. Everyone did a really good job of trying to cut across socioeconomic lines [and] race lines, and it was a very, very well put together group that really had good representation." Leon Kaplan describes his experience in the American Leadership Forum as promoting "a good sense of how to involve and enroll and work with a variety of people." Characterizing one of the most successful broad-based collaboration efforts in recent history, the Newark Collaboration Group, Saul Fenster states, "One of the things we concluded early on was what you do *not* do. You do not form a blue-ribbon panel to create a report with recommendations, which will sit on a shelf and not be implemented. Those reports fill libraries all over the United States. They are of absolutely no impact whatever. So the whole issue of empowerment came into play." Another participant says, "Our philosophy is, if you have people around the table who can make things happen—and those who can stop it from happening—then it will happen."

A similar consensus has emerged among those who facilitate or study the collaborative process. Chris Gates of the National Civic League puts it this way:

In the days when citizens gave up their proxy to large institutional players, they did so in part because they did not feel as if they had enough information to form a balanced judgement on the issue at hand. Now, because of the information revolution that has taken place in this country, many more citizens feel they have enough information to be directly involved in the resolution of issues. What all of this has meant for communities is that they are full of people who have just enough power to say "no." The goal for the 1990s must be to find ways to also say "yes" in this new environment where everyone expects a seat at the table [1991, p. 118].

Following a foundation-sponsored review of research literature on factors influencing successful collaboration, Paul Mattessich and Barbara Monsey conclude that "the collaborative group includes representatives from each segment of the community who will be affected by its activities" (1992, p. 20). As we noted in previous chapters, that was our experience as well: broad-based involvement was present in every case of successful collaboration we examined. Yet many problem-solving efforts begin with the opposite intent.

Some initiators of a "problem-solving process" spend a lot of time talking about who should *not* be invited to the meeting, who should be excluded from the process, how to keep information and communication from reaching certain people or groups, and strategies designed to frustrate and block those who are seen as the "opposition." These exclusion strategies often fail. In fact, James Coleman's research shows that opposition in dealing with community problems can create polarizations that make matters worse, resulting in a problem that is more difficult to solve (1989, pp. 330–340).

The incredible difficulties involved in creating and sustaining collaboration may tempt leaders to simplify the process. They may want to take shortcuts to avoid the frustrations that come from bringing out and dealing with very divergent points of view. And this desire to avoid arguments, clear differences of opinion, the tensions that accompany disagreements, and the time it takes to manage differences often causes people to make a fundamental error in initiating collaboration: that error is to be exclusive rather than inclusive.

If broad-based involvement is a key feature of successful collaboration, then there is one particularly important implication. The review of the literature on research into factors influencing successful collaboration that was mentioned earlier states the conclusion this way: "At the very beginning of an effort, collaborating partners should temporarily set aside the purpose of the collaboration and devote energy to learning about each other" (Mattessich and Monsey, 1992, p. 19). Another summary of research (Goldberg and Larson, 1992) identifies this same factor, called "informal exploring." Informal exploring gives the stakeholders valuable time to get to know each other, to discuss interests, to appreciate the points of view and values that are common to members of the group, and to share hopes and fears. Do not begin the process by creating advocates. Keep positions from emerging quickly and hardening. Trust and the willingness to listen take time to grow, especially in groups whose membership crosses boundaries that have traditionally fostered lack of understanding and mistrust. Informal exploring is critical in the early stages of collaboration. Its importance is reinforced by the second basic principal for initiating successful collaboration.

Create a Credible, Open Process

At the beginning of almost any broad-based collaborative process, there is suspicion and cynicism. Participants ask themselves a lot of questions: What is *really* going on here? Who is really behind this? What strings are being pulled? Have the decisions already been made? Whose interests are being served? This underlying public mood of cynicism and mistrust regarding government, politics, and public policy issues has been well documented. Surveys and polls repeatedly disclose that the average citizen has little confidence in any institution. A true expert on public opinion, Lee Atwater, the recently deceased past chairman of the Republican Party, stated that "the American people are cynical and turned off about all the institutions, and politics is one. Bull permeates everything. In other words, my theory is that the American people think politics and politicians are full of baloney. They think the media and journalists are full of baloney. They think organized religion is full of baloney. They think big business is full of baloney. They think big labor is full of baloney. To single out politics is making a grave mistake in terms of understanding attitudes of Americans" (Oreskes, 1990, p. A22).

Within this climate of cynicism, people are asked to get involved in a collaborative effort. Whether they become involved, how much energy is invested in their effort, and how much collaborative involvement is sustained over time depend to a large degree on how they see the process in which they are involved. If it is a credible process (that is, it has both integrity and a fair chance of producing results) and an open process (that is, the dialogue is both honest and receptive to different points of view), then people will invest the energy—the enormous expenditure of energy necessary to make collaboration succeed. Creating and nurturing this open and credible process is extraordinarily important for those who are initiating collaboration.

A particularly good example of a credible, open process is that which was created for the Denver Bond Project. Consider how those involved in the project describe the process. First, Mayor Federico Peña: "I said, 'Look, we're not going to do a disservice to this work by politicizing the issue.' This is a citizen group, and if they think that these are the ten most important priorities of the city, let's go get them. Let's go do them. I'm not going to sit there and then second-guess them and say, 'Well, no, I want the library put on it this year.' I wanted to give them respect, credibility. I said, 'All right, not only will I accept your decisions, I'm going to go out and support you and campaign for you.'"

Tim Sandos, one of the co-chairs of the citizen group, sees it this way: "Our process was so open and so inclusive, it created credibility for the media. This wasn't just a group of people handpicked to do the mayor's bidding, or to rubber-stamp what was being passed on to them. We brought in our own proposals that the city had nothing to do with. We fought with the city. And that created the credibility. There were people that were housewives. There were people that were Little League coaches. There were attorneys. There were doctors. There were public people and private people. Just a broad cross-section of folks, and that brought credibility."

The other co-chair, Harry Lewis, says, "There wasn't an overtly political agenda there, other than the one that most of us recognized was there. Initially, there was some concern by a few of the committee members that we were going to be used as a rubber stamp. I spoke directly to that, as did a number of other people on the committee. Essentially, I stated that if I thought I was being used as a rubber stamp, I wouldn't be here. I tried to empower the committee to be totally independent in their approach, which I think they were."

The chair of the transportation subcommittee, Lee White, says, "I think that the first meeting I went to I was skeptical and said, 'This isn't really going to get anywhere.' But pretty soon, people began to realize that they had genuinely been empowered to do this, and that this was not a futile exercise with a needless manifest, and that the mayor and the council were really hoping that this thing worked. About four weeks into the process, the committee began to say, 'Hey, we're not being dominated by the technocrats. We really are being asked to decide all these things, so we'll take it seriously.'"

Steve Welchert, a consultant on the project, recalls the process: "The public saw the committee cutting the budget. They saw it in a very public process. It was very painful for a lot of community people to be involved in. Here you are looking at probably $200 million of unmet needs in Parks and Recreation. What finally made it to the ballot was $50 million. So they had to cut a hundred-plus million dollars of very needy, very worthy items. A lot of worthy things got sliced out of this package. That was a fairly painful process. It was a public budget debate, but it was important for us to put that on the floor. Let everybody see that this wasn't a committee that was about wish lists, and it wasn't a committee that was about getting *everything* done that 'needed' to get done. It was a committee that was about getting done what we had to get done. The absolute essentials, to keep our city healthy and moving forward. This wasn't frivolous. It wasn't a lot of fluff. These were very serious, hard-core, needed projects."

According to an expert evaluator of collaborative efforts, Chris Gates of the National Civic League, "This was a very diverse group—an extremely diverse group—which I thought was important. The city had the guts to actually turn control of the process over to the citizens, and they did not have a hidden agenda, and they did not keep control behind the scenes with 'strings.' And then the city council had the guts to more or less accept the report. They made some minor fine-tuning changes, but you know, the worst thing that can happen in a process like this is that citizens go do all this work and then the council says, 'Thanks,' and nothing happens. And then people get angry. But they had the guts to stay with it, and that's hard to do sometimes, for elected officials."

Leaders attempting to create a credible, open process must remember the key factors brought out in these interview quotes. Accomplishing the objective is more important than who is in charge. Making good decisions is more important than whose interests are served. Being open is more important than projecting a "good image." Keeping behind-the-scenes activity minimal to nonexistent is essential. Gaining a commitment to the results of the process from stakeholders from the very beginning lets the people involved in the process know that their effort will amount to something.

Though the specifics varied, these fundamental aspects of the collaborative process were present in all of the cases of successful collaboration that we studied.

Promote Visible Support from Acknowledged Leaders

In an analysis of specific cases of successful international collaboration, Harlan Cleveland describes one of the necessary conditions:

> *Individuals make things happen.* In the early stages of each of these success stories, a crucial role was played by a few key individuals who acted (whatever payroll they were on) as international people in leading, pushing, insisting, inspiring, sharing knowledge, and generating a climate of trust that brushed off the distrust still prevailing in other domains. On the World Weather Watch these were mostly scientific statesmen; on small pox eradication, public health

officers; on the Law of the Sea, visionary lawyers, including key players from the developing world; on outer space cooperation, lawyers
and later some of the space travelers themselves with their visions
of an undivided earth; on the frequency spectrum, a few telecom-
munications experts who saw an interconnected world that cooperation could create and conflict could destroy [1990–1991, p. 15].

In every example of successful collaboration we encountered,
there were people who served as catalysts—one or more people
who had the clear vision, or the energy to get people moving, or
the words to inspire imagination, or the influence to marshal the
resources, or simply the nerve to call the meeting. In the beginning, collaboration is fueled by individual acts.

Arnie Graf, lead organizer for the BUILD organization,
describes an event he considers instrumental in the success of the
Baltimore Commonwealth Project: "Bob Keller agreed to come to
Brown's Memorial Baptist Church, which is in a lower-income area
of Park Heights, and talk to about 1,500 people. And he came. You
know, you just don't see white people down there, and you certainly
don't see white people of his stature. The fact that he came, I mean
it had an enormously emotional value and said something to people in a way that they hadn't heard before. And I think Bob did it
not only because it would be symbolic or whatever, but I think Bob
wanted to show people that he had a commitment to work on this
problem. His spirit in his talk was evident. It was one of those special evenings you don't get a chance to participate in very often."

Every successful collaboration project is driven initially by individual effort. Alex Plinio's efforts on behalf of the Newark Collaboration Group, Terry Goddard's efforts on behalf of the Phoenix
Futures Forum, and Federico Peña's efforts on behalf of the Citizens for Denver's Future, for example, were critical in terms of getting the projects going. The visible commitment of people who are
thought of as "leaders" is very important, especially in the early

stages. Collaborative projects that have the early support of highly visible leaders are much more likely to succeed.

There is an interesting addendum to this pattern. In research on unusually successful volunteer organizations, Catherine Sweeney (1990) found a similar pattern. What inspired and motivated the volunteers in these organizations was not the staff of professional volunteer coordinators. Instead, it was the officers and leaders of the formal organization that the volunteers were working with. If the leaders of the organization were highly visible, articulating the goals in ways that inspired the volunteers—if they were out there where they could be seen getting their hands dirty—the volunteer organization produced unusual outcomes.

In the early stages of collaboration, the visible commitment of "leaders"—commitment not just to renewal but to the specific *process* they have initiated—encourages participants, adds importance to the goals of the project, and increases confidence in the process. In addition, this commitment gives people hope that what they are doing has support outside their own group, that even though the problem is complex and the resources required to address it are considerable, it still might be possible to do something about it.

Seek Support from or Gain the Acquiescence of Established Authorities

One of the co-chairs of the group Citizens for Denver's Future, Tim Sandos, reminds us of a pragmatic issue in many collaborative projects: "Keep in mind that we were only advisory to city council. We had to take our decisions to city council, and they had the option to change, delete, or add to our proposal in any fashion they saw fit. Well, because we had worked with city council throughout the entire process, it was fairly well established by the time we got to their door that they were going to take all or most of what we had."

A similar narrative comes from Earl Reynolds, discussing the Roanoke Vision: "The city manager bought in early, to the extent that he was even willing to incur the wrath of other folks in the organization, on the operational side, because the only money he had to give us was what he could take out of equipment purchases. There were some people in this organization who were real hot about that, because they understand buying trucks, but they don't understand the future. So he had to take some risk; he had to take some flack."

Dennis Burke, an active citizen participant in the Phoenix Futures Forum, attributes much of the ultimate success of that project to "the new mayor, his name is Paul Johnson. He has done what we really didn't expect he would do, which was read all this stuff and fall in love with it. He actually said, 'Let's do it.' And he assigned each member of the city council a separate area of implementation. And citizen task forces were appointed for each of those areas, and a remarkable amount of progress has already been made in terms of weaving these recommendations into the existing process of city government."

If you were a citizen-based initiative working to keep kids from dropping out of public schools, you probably would not expect a whole lot of resistance from the public schools themselves. But resistance from the public schools is exactly what the Baltimore Commonwealth encountered. For most people involved in a collaborative effort, the goal is so clear and so worthwhile that the ultimate realities of eventually working with other people in other agencies to implement the plans, proposals, or initiatives growing out of the collaborative project fade into the background. But those realities are there. Successful collaborative efforts recognize those realities early in the process. The groundwork is laid early and nurtured throughout the process. The individuals or agencies recognized as necessarily involved in the action or implementation stage are brought in at the beginning, and they are invited to participate in the process to whatever extent they wish. We were intrigued by the discovery that many of the most successful cases of broad-based collaboration were initiated by private citizens. The Newark Collaboration Group was initiated by Alex Plinio. What is now the American Leadership Forum was initiated by Joe Jaworski. The Baltimore Commonwealth was initiated by two citizen groups (the Greater Baltimore Committee and Baltimoreans United in Leadership Development). All of these are examples of citizens who were unwilling to wait for leadership to come from political and institutional leaders.

Initiating a Collaborative Process

In the initial phase of a collaborative endeavor, the leadership task is to build agreement among stakeholders that problems exist and then to get enough of those stakeholders to agree to work together in a constructive way. Attempts to gain agreement on problem definition, solutions, and implementation are premature without these basic understandings.

In Phoenix, newspaper publisher Pat Murphy took on the task of convincing citizens that the city's problems needed to be addressed. In 1986 he asked *Washington Post* columnist Neal Peirce to prepare, with other urban professionals, "a fresh and untinted view of our problems and opportunities." His purpose was to "stir the community to write an agenda for action" (Hall and Weschler, 1991, p. 141). In February of 1987, 500,000 residents read the results of Peirce's penetrating analysis in the city's two major newspapers. The "Peirce Report" vividly portrayed the city's problems and presented a compelling case for action. The widespread attention and concern generated by the report meant that Phoenix's problems could no longer be ignored. The following year, Mayor Terry Goddard initiated the Phoenix Futures Forum, a highly participative, collaborative approach to creating a vision and a strategic plan for the city that would help cope with the problems of growth.

Creating or recognizing a clear need is not enough by itself. Someone has to recognize the appropriate timing and move to act, just as Mayor Goddard did in Phoenix. In Newark, as we have noted, the city's enormous problems were all too clear. The task was to find out if a sufficient number of the city's key stakeholders had enough energy and concern to address the problems in a comprehensive and systematic fashion. To accomplish that task, Alex Plinio began his interviews of a broad cross-section of the city's leaders. He wanted two questions answered: First, was there enough leadership and leadership commitment to warrant trying to bring the community together in a productive way? Second, was it worth the risk to even try? The strong affirmations Plinio received led to the first meetings of what became the Newark Collaboration Group (NCG). With widespread recognition of Newark's problems and a commitment to work together, NCG's leaders could begin to explore how to work together constructively.

Many collaborative initiatives are begun by a small group of people with the credibility to convince others that something can and must be done. The members of these "initiating committees," as they are often called, are broadly representative of the larger community. Their tasks are to identify the stakeholders, design a credible process, ensure that good information is available, identify and recruit leaders who can promote and safeguard the process, and find the resources (staff, process design expertise, facilitators, dollars, and so on) to carry out a collaborative process. Their presence assures other citizens that the process will be fair, inclusive, and well informed. Since one or a few people rarely have the credibility to convince others of the fairness of the process, these groups usually have eight to fifteen members. The key question in setting up an initiating committee is this: Does the membership have the credibility to get people to agree that problems exist and to work together to address them? Specifically, the tasks of an initiating committee are these:

- Identify stakeholders.
- Design the collaborative process and timeline.
- Determine information and education needs.
- Identify and recruit credible leaders who can promote and safeguard the process.
- Identify resource needs—for example, process design expertise, facilitation expertise, staff support, and financial resources.
- Gain agreement of stakeholders to participate.

Most individuals who want to start a collaborative initiative are energized and committed but are nevertheless intimidated or overwhelmed by the enormity and complexity of the problem. With the help of others in the initiating role (and with careful attention to the fundamentals), however, it is possible for citizens and civic leaders alike to spark successful projects that can lead to meaningful, sustainable change.

Chapter Six

Building and Sustaining Momentum

Sustaining broad-based collaborative initiatives is a difficult challenge. In one of the most complete summaries of what is known about collaboration, Barbara Gray discusses six issues that must be addressed during the early phases of collaboration (1989, pp. 57–74):

1. A common definition of the problem, including how this problem relates to the interdependence of parties or organizations. (Many of the cases in our research involved problems that defied "definition." While there was broad agreement that a problem or problems existed in these cases, there was little agreement on a common definition of the problem[s].)
2. A commitment to collaborate, growing from the interests of the stakeholders and the building and maintenance of trust among both present and potential participants.
3. The identification of other stakeholders whose involvement is important.
4. The acceptance of the legitimacy of other stakeholders.
5. The presence of a convener to bring the parties together (an issue we will discuss at greater length in Chapter Eight, "Skills for a New Kind of Leadership").
6. The identification of resources that are needed for the collaboration to proceed.

As these issues get raised and dealt with, leaders and participants in successful collaborative initiatives promote and sustain the process in three principle ways. First, trust among stakeholders is essential and must be built in order that the collaborating group can find and expand common interests. Second, the process must be protected by patient, principled, skillful leadership. Third, the common purpose must be aggressively articulated and pursued to elevate the common goal to a clear and compelling status.

Building Trust

In order to sustain collaboration for the long haul, a climate of trust and openness is essential. In the beginning, that climate usually does not exist. Stakeholders bring other concerns, such as narrowly defined parochial agendas and predetermined positions about acceptable outcomes. The natural tendency of the parties, in terms of agenda setting and behavior, is to start with differences rather than with common ground. Differences are easily magnified, which further undermines trust and leads quickly to failure. Building a collaborative climate and sustaining it through the many difficult and frustrating moments that lie ahead demands a solid foundation of trust. There are several ways to build trust. We turn to these now.

Informal Exploring

The principle of informal exploring has been recognized in studies of what successful negotiators do (Goldberg and Larson, 1992). It requires an investment of time in getting the parties acquainted with each other, exploring interests, sharing perspectives on the problem, and avoiding the dangerous "lock-ins" that occur when people advocate the positions of the organizations or groups that they represent. The need for this component of trust building was crystallized by several of the people that we talked to. Earl Reynolds, for example, discusses the obstacles that had to be overcome in Roanoke Vision, a long-range planning effort: "By its nature, planning is theoretical, and it doesn't endorse collaborative planning. People in the profession aren't taught collaborative planning in the halls of academia, and in most communities that they go to work in, there's no collaborative planning going on; so they don't learn it. It's confrontation. Planning is always confrontation."

A member of the Newark Collaboration Group found that "the biggest obstacle was deprogramming, getting away from a preset agenda. People would come in to the meetings and try to railroad an agenda through. We had to dismantle that immediately. We really had to find a different style of working." This different style of working takes more time and patience than most people are accustomed to expending. But its role in determining the success of a broad-based collaborative effort is clear.

Junius Williams, of the Newark Collaboration Group, describes the major obstacle encountered in the early phases of that effort: "The main [problem] was getting people to trust each other. People didn't have the experience of working together, and when they had come together, it had been on a confrontational basis. So this was another way to come together to solve problems, and people weren't used to that. The business community didn't trust the 'militants.' The community people were concerned about being left out of whatever decision-making process was established. It was a matter of people not knowing each other. So it's a matter of coming to know each other and trust each other and as a result of that trying to find a common denominator around which people could work. That was the biggest problem."

Trust takes time to develop, especially among diverse people who are not used to working together; but the time is well spent. Rather than allowing people to move in the direction of making speeches, engaging in debate, or making motions and voting on them, groups can be more productive if they actively promote exploration. The exploration can be of each other's backgrounds, perspectives on the problems, or interests; it can be of values, priorities, issues that need to be discussed, and so forth. This exploration can occur in a variety of ways. Consider the following two examples.

Bob Keller, of the Baltimore Commonwealth, talks about the early stages in the relationship between the two primary organizations, GBC and BUILD, from which the Baltimore Commonwealth eventually grew: "[BUILD] wanted a major commitment around job training and jobs. So we danced with them on it for a long time. It never really got ugly. It got a little tense, but it never really got ugly. We were making no ostensible progress. What we were doing, however, was establishing some credibility with one another—getting to know one another, probing, doing all that kind of stuff. And there was a meeting, and the Boston Compact idea was put on the table; and so we had switched from job training to education. Here was a place where GBC had a commitment, BUILD had a commitment, and we began to see some real possibility. That started the negotiating process."

A different kind of process worked for the Newark Collaboration Group. Ken Gibson describes the process that was followed by David Straus of Interaction Associates, who facilitated the process: "Well, what they did was they get these guys who come in with the big charts, right? Eighteen different little Magic Markers in their hands. They stand up there, and they say, 'What do you think is the most important issue?' He gets garbage on the streets over here, and he gets transportation for the employees over there, which is a completely different kind of situation. Pretty soon you've got a lot of things down. Sooner or later, somebody from the business community will say something that's also important to the guy over here, and those are the things you start to work on first. Common areas of interest. So sooner or later, there's a little meeting of the ways. Well, here's a place to start."

Informal exploring is an important step in promoting collaboration. The opportunity to discover common interests, similar ways of defining the problem, and shared aspirations for solutions, as well as the opportunity to get to know individuals as people, is important enough that it must be deliberately built into the process for working together.

Sharing Ownership

We have suggested several times that people are often cynical and mistrustful in the early stages of a broad-based collaborative effort. These attributes become evident as the group begins to deal with initial control and ownership issues. Who decides when we meet? Who decides what the agenda is? How do we make decisions? Do we decide by consensus, majority vote, or something else? All sorts of these procedural issues will arise early in the process. For collaboration to work, participants must take ownership of these issues and create a consensus about how to move ahead. The more participants take ownership of the process, the more sustainable the collaborative effort will be.

In the successful efforts, those who provided the initial leadership very quickly and systematically transferred ownership to the participants themselves. Harry Lewis, one of the co-leaders of the Denver Bond Project, states, "Ownership is not that important. I figured this is the city's agenda, so I'm just going to let it play out. All Tim [Sandos] and I did was steer the boat to try to keep from running up on a sandbar. We just tried to keep the process going and shepherd that process so that the committee could decide what they wanted to do."

One of the participants in Roanoke Vision describes the leadership provided by Earl Reynolds: "Earl was just an incredible guy in terms of building this collaborative process and empowering. Back then the word *empowerment* wasn't a word that most people understood. In the late seventies and early eighties, if neighborhoods were empowered there was clearly the belief that government had to give up something. But as we started through this process, there was a real paradigm shift for us to let go and simply try and create a forum or an atmosphere for this discussion to take place."

Leon Kaplan, discussing his experience with the American Leadership Forum, states, "What I got was a really good sense of how to involve and enroll and work with a variety of people with diverse perspectives. I still try to do that. I'm still cognizant of that as an issue, and I'm aware within myself that I have to give up my ownership of things, knowing that there might be a better way to do something."

Alex Plinio, recognized as having exercised remarkable leadership in starting the Newark Collaboration Group, was asked what obstacles he encountered in initiating that collaboration. His response:

Certainly the first and most difficult obstacle was the level of trust. That was a key impediment. Trust had to increase. The lack of trust, in effect, slowed things down. It was the key, I think, to a lot of it. Trust. Here's a good anecdote. There was a large YMCA that has been around for a number of years. At the time when we had finished the first leaders' meeting and we were going to widen the group, I was sitting in the mayor's outer office waiting to see him, and the head of the Y came out. He said to me, "I hear that you had a meeting of leaders and I wasn't invited. I think that it's about time for some of us nonprofits to organize. I'm getting a group of leaders together," and so on. This was a problem of trust. So my response to him was the value system adopted early by the collaboration: one of openness and inclusiveness. I apologized for the oversight, telling him that he should have been invited, that he *is* included, and that we would like him to be a leader and to be among this group. I asked him to bring any of the other leaders he wanted to with him to the next meeting. He came.

Another example is we would put as many people "up front" as possible. Not the leadership of the collaboration, but the leadership of the city. We were not to become a shadow government, for example, but to give credit to council persons, mayors, heads of colleges, neighborhood groups, etc. This is the exact opposite of what most organizations do early on; they try to attract credit for themselves. You should do just the opposite. Give it away. Don't claim credit. Be sure that someone else gets it, whoever is working on it or is at the center of it.

There is an underlying point of view in the attitudes of these leaders: stay away from ownership issues for yourself and your organization; instead, create ownership of the process and the outcomes for the participants themselves. Recognize that ownership resides in everyone involved in the process. The only consensus that really matters is that of the stakeholders—all of them.

Celebrating Success

A more subtle factor that impacts the maintenance of a trusting, collaborative climate has to do with the enormous complexity of the problems typically addressed by collaborations. If a problem seems so overwhelming that people question their effectiveness in dealing with it, they may become impatient with the progress they are making.

In our research, we noticed that successful collaborations frequently celebrated their interim successes. Reaching a milestone in the project, overcoming a particularly difficult obstacle, attracting substantial new resources, bringing heretofore-resistant new partners into the collaboration—these were all reasons for celebrating success. The celebrations ranged from large banquets to small pizza parties, from press conferences to coffee and doughnuts. Their common theme was a recognition of progress. Participants often later identified these celebrations as particular events or points in time when they became encouraged, when their spirits were lifted, or when they recognized the emergence of a special relationship with other members of the collaborative effort. Small successes along the way were crucial to sustaining the energy of the collaboration.

Creating Powerful, Impelling Experiences

Powerful, impelling experiences can be used to quickly develop a deep level of trust and respect among stakeholders. A shared experience of this kind can transform a collection of individuals into a group and unify them around a set of values and a common purpose. The American Leadership Forum provides such an experience for the diverse individuals who make up an "ALF class" within a given community. At the beginning of each new class, the members attend a six-day "wilderness challenge," originally conducted by the Colorado Outward Bound School. This deeply humanizing experience is described by ALF members as the major reason for the high level of trust and respect they have for each other. Their solid relationships sustain them through difficult times and allow them to focus on the broader concerns of the community, secure in the knowledge that their narrower interests will be considered and respected. Impelling experiences are especially helpful in the early stages of collaborative groups. Any experience—whether river rafting, rock climbing, or some other team-building activity—that strengthens common bonds and renders individual differences less important can help sustain the energy to work together.

Actively Leading the Process

Leadership plays a critical role in sustaining collaboration. Recent research on collaboration (Roberts and Bradley, 1991) underscores a key feature: it is a very interactive process. Collaboration involves sustained, self-critical interaction among participants. Nancy

Roberts and Raymond Bradley remind us that "virtually all aspects of the process are open to constant reexamination and reevaluation" (p. 212). Collaboration is a self-reflective, evolving process that must be aggressively promoted and constantly nurtured. And even though it is constantly changing and evolving, its fundamental principles must be protected.

We usually think of leaders as those who articulate a vision, inspire people to act, and focus on concrete problems and results. Collaboration needs a different kind of leadership; it needs leaders who can safeguard the process, facilitate interaction, and patiently deal with high levels of frustration. Collaboration works when there are a few key leaders, either in formal or informal roles, who keep the process going.

Safeguarding the Process

Creating and sustaining a credible and open process is everyone's responsibility, to be sure, but successful collaborations also have one person (or a few people) who promotes, values, and protects the openness and credibility of the process. Many participants in the Phoenix Futures Forum identified Herb Ely as that person and credited his strong process leadership for much of the success of that project. Linda DeAtley states, "My expectations weren't very high at first. I just wanted to let people know about the Arizona Heritage Fair, and then I saw that people really were sincerely committed to making this process work. Everybody's opinion had value and was recognized. I think Herb Ely was really the core of it, and I think he deserves the credit. He always made sure that everybody was recognized and included."

Bob Herbert, of Roanoke Vision, expresses a similar sentiment: "A comprehensive plan was something you learn about in graduate school—something that we need to do, technically under state law, every five years. Nobody understood that this was really a major community project. Like if you've never been in love, people tell you what it's like to be in love, and you go, 'Well, I guess I understand.' Then you fall in love and go, 'Wow, is *this* what they're talking about?' No one could fully appreciate what Earl [Reynolds] was talking about. Sometimes you had to grab people by the back of the neck and say, 'Hey, look what's going on here.'"

After describing some special-interest pressures that threatened the ultimate success of Citizens for Denver's Future, reporter Suzanne Weis commented, "Lewis [the co-chair] held on and was backed by other members of the committee. And what he said was, 'We've been committed to a process all along that's inclusive and relies on consensus. We're not going to let this whole thing go up in smoke. We agreed on how we would do things, and we're going to hold to the integrity of the process.'"

Facilitating the Process

Strong process leadership not only focuses on safeguarding the process by adhering to the principles of collaboration; it is also concerned with *facilitating* the process. Whether the expertise comes from the members themselves or from professional facilitators, effective facilitation is necessary for the initiative to work.

Joyce Kroeller says of the Baltimore Commonwealth, "You've got to have a couple of leaders. There's a formal chair, but you've got to have a couple of people who facilitate as well. When the group gets off track, you need someone who can frame the right question or bring the group back to the point. It may not always be the same person, but we have a couple of people who do that very well."

One of the original members of the Newark Collaboration Group discusses what she sees as one of the most important reasons for the success of that collaboration: "It was important that they had a really good consultant at the beginning, with the Interaction Associates people. Board members who were there at the beginning said it would have fallen apart if it hadn't been for them. And I think that's true in general. You have to have a good process, and then you can move to product and results."

Bob Herbert sees the primary reason for the success of Roanoke Vision as this: "We brought in a team of consultants to assist the community in this effort. It was expensive, but it was clearly one of the key reasons why Roanoke Vision succeeded. The consultant team members were primarily communicators, and they were real people, not people who were 'buttoned-down.' Citizens could really relate to them. They knew how to communicate."

The cases we analyzed illustrated two complementary aspects of process leadership: a visible commitment to the principles of a credible and open process and the ability to facilitate or to provide facilitation. A third aspect of process leadership, practicing patience, underlies these first two.

Practicing Patience

Strong process leadership necessarily involves patience. Participants in collaborative processes frequently describe them as very long and very frustrating. If you have ever been involved in a collaborative process, you undoubtedly understand what we are talking about. Consider the following excerpts from just two of our interviews.

Linda Harris says of the Baltimore Commonwealth, "We had a whole year of people trying to build the trust necessary to pull something like this together. It was meetings every two weeks— very frustrating meetings, because everyone had their own identity, had their own programs, had things they were afraid they would lose in the process of developing the strategy. We all sat around the table from the beginning. And it's been almost the same set of people from the very beginning. It was a consensus process that took painstaking time to build."

Saul Fenster discusses the Newark Collaboration Group experience: "What got me impatient, as a person who sometimes shows certain directive tendencies, was the endless process that went into determining what the process would be. We hired facilitators at pretty good rates to facilitate meetings for the first couple of years. In the first few meetings—I don't remember how long this went on—we actually had photographs taken of the materials that the facilitators put on the charts on the wall so that no one would say that the minutes had been in some way doctored. That's called trust building. So we went through this tedious process. Maybe that was the most stressful part of it, even before we got started: deciding how we would operate. And the facilitators were extremely important, because they could be very patient. So we would meet them in the room, and the room would be surrounded by these papers hanging on the wall. Someone would say, 'Wait a minute, I didn't say that. Cross it out. What I said was X,' and it would be crossed out."

Strong process leadership is a very valuable commodity. It is so rare that organizations have been built to provide it or develop it. Collaboration cannot succeed unless there are a few people whose primary attention is on making the process work.

Pursuing the Common Goal

The final fundamental principle in sustaining collaboration is a subtle one that continues to be debated in theories of collective action. For decades scholars and reflective practitioners have discussed "integration" versus "differentiation"; they have puzzled over the question of how self-interest can be aligned with common interests in achieving any group's, organization's, or society's objectives.

We know that collaboration can succeed even when individuals focus primarily on their own self-interest (Wood and Gray, 1991). We also know that extraordinary outcomes in collective efforts are possible when the group objective is considered more important than any individual's objectives (Larson and LaFasto, 1989). This does not mean that the individuals do not pursue self-interests; it simply means that individual self-interests are seen as obtainable through the achievement of the group's goals.

In order for collaboration to occur in the first place, the participants must believe that the collaboration will serve their own interests. But as the process evolves, and as the emotional energy that helps sustain the initiative through difficult times develops, there is a shift from narrow, parochial concerns to broader, communal concerns. This shift is often described as occurring at a specific time or around a particular event. Once it occurs, it is actively promoted and reinforced by the group. This shift is a profound one, and it marks a turning point in the life of a collaborative initiative.

In the Phoenix Futures Forum, this shift occurred in the norms that surrounded the small-group meetings. Initially, people tended to speak as representatives of particular interests or organizations. But a norm quickly developed wherein speakers were told—sometimes were *interrupted* to be told—"We're not interested in what you believe as a representative of X; we want to know what you think as a citizen of Phoenix." Members of the Phoenix Futures Forum identified this norm as a profound shift in the nature and quality of the collaboration that followed.

If we turn to what is reported by members of some of the other successful collaborative efforts, perhaps we can better understand the character of this profound shift in focus from individual to common interests. Citizens for Denver's Future was one of the cases initially most likely to promote the pursuit of individual interests. CDF's task, you will remember, involved the allocation of funds for specific improvement and renovation projects in various parts of the city.

Tim Sandos, one of the co-chairs of CDF's citizen group, recalls the early phases of that task: "We brought them all together and said, . . . 'We want you to forget what neighborhood you come from, and the reason we want you to do that is because we want you to look at this more broadly.' What's in the best interest of the entire city, not just your own little neighborhood? And don't get into these subcommittees and get into a fight to protect the park that's across the street from your home. You have to look at what's going to be fair for everyone in the city."

The other co-chair of this project, Harry Lewis, describes the maintenance of this broader perspective throughout the project: "Occasionally, we heard hints of, 'If you don't vote for my project, I ain't gonna vote for your project.' We constantly preached to our executive committee that we had to put neighborhood interests aside and really look at the entire city's interests. We said, 'If we get into vote sharing or swapping, we'll end up with the worst of all possible solutions.' We had to take a broad perspective on the total city. And by and large, I think we were very successful in achieving that."

Promoting or encouraging this profound shift in perspectives is a difficult thing to do. Many people show up for collective action convinced that their primary job is to advocate only for the narrow interests of their own constituents. In fact, many of the collaborative efforts we have experienced have not gotten beyond this perspective.

As we have noted, a focus on narrow interests often characterizes the early stages of a collaborative effort. Charlie Hancock, of Roanoke Vision, comments, "I think we worked more as individuals when we first got together. We thought that the individual groups better get their 'pitch' in fast. We met, and met, and met; and as time went on, this began to change." Glynn Barranger, also of Roanoke Vision, remembers the situation in similar terms: "I think, like any committee of this nature, the members at first were concerned with the problems they had where they lived. After the group worked together for a while, then we became concerned about problems within the entire city."

The way the profound shift occurs varies considerably from case to case. To get a feel for some of the subtleties of this shift, consider the following examples. Linda Harris, of the Baltimore Commonwealth, says, "There were lots of existing programs with funding, with constituents, with an identity. All of us knew that if we were going to bring things together under the umbrella of the Commonwealth (at that time we didn't have a name), people had to give up the images that they had spent a great deal of time cultivating for the separate programs. I think that was a very big hurdle that had to be overcome in the beginning. A *very* big hurdle."

Another participant adds, "It just moved from a *we/they* to an *us*. And that even came out in language. People would say, 'They want to . . . ,' and someone would say, 'Wait a minute; you're talking about us.' That started to happen, actually, about two years ago."

George Hampton vividly recalls his own experience of this shift during his work with the Newark Collaboration Group: "It was about a year or two after I started, when going to the plenary meetings and simply seeing the so-called major stakeholders in the same room with the poorest in the city, dealing with issues. They were talking about the Newark Education Council, prior to actually establishing the NEC. In the same room you had the president of Newark Teachers Union, the chairman of the board of education for the city, the superintendent of schools, all three of them in the same room—when prior to that they were always pulling, battling among themselves on issues. Together, same room at the same time, willing to discuss education alongside people from state government, alongside Mrs. Jones, who was worried about her son getting out of Camden Street School. They were just sitting there participating like anybody else. That was one big day."

A similar shift is described in some interesting research by Jeanne Logsdon (Logsdon, 1991), who describes two dynamic patterns of collaboration formation, either of which may increase collaboration. One pattern is from interdependence to interest. This pattern involves parties who first recognize that they are mutually involved in a problem and then subsequently experience a shift from low to high stakes. As the problem intensifies—perhaps conditions change or a threat to the well-being of the parties comes from some outside common source—their interest in working out a joint solution increases. The parties first recognize themselves as interdependent, and then their interest in collaborating increases.

The second pattern, interests to interdependence, happens when the interests of the parties move from low to high first, and then the perceived interdependence shifts from low to high. Logsdon describes a case in Silicon Valley, when in 1980 and 1981 "five large high-technology firms independently discovered chemical leaks from tanks or piping systems into the soil" (p. 33). The discovery of the leaks raised the interests from low to high in each of the five firms individually. The subsequent discovery that other firms had experienced the same problem raised the perceived interdependence from low to high.

When the kinds of profound shifts we are talking about occur during the collaboration process, they are described by the participants as accompanied by changes in language behavior, in the norms of the group, in the perception of decreased or nonexistent differences in power and status, and in other factors that signal a shift from narrow, parochial interests to broader, collective interests. Building and sustaining a collaborative climate for the long run depends on promoting and encouraging these shifts.

In our exemplary cases of collaboration, these shifts occurred "naturally." But we believe that they can be actively promoted. They are fostered by the first two factors we discussed in this chapter: building trust and exhibiting strong process leadership. There is clear evidence, especially in the Newark Collaboration Group and in Citizens for Denver's Future, that these shifts can be actively encouraged and persuasively promoted by leaders of collaborative efforts.

Realizing the Benefits of Collaboration

Promoting and sustaining the collaborative process creates the conditions for diverse groups of citizens to be able to create shared visions, define problems, and generate solutions. While there are many techniques and strategies for collaborative visioning and problem solving, in order to get results all must be supported by the practices we have described thus far.

Chapter Seven

Producing Results that Matter

Successful collaboration produces results, not just structures and activities that create the illusion that a problem is being addressed. The results are both tangible (in terms of impacting the problem) and developmental (in terms of empowering citizens and creating changes in how communities "do business" around public concerns).

The Measure of Success

Most definitions of leadership focus implicitly on creating useful change; leaders are defined as successful when their actions lead to meaningful, sustainable results. Political scientist and historian James Macgregor Burns says, in his groundbreaking book *Leadership,* "The effectiveness of leaders must be judged not by their press clippings but by actual social change measured by intent and by the satisfaction of human needs and expectations" (1978, p. 3). John Kotter, a Harvard Business School professor, labels leadership effective "when it moves people to a place in which both they and those who depend upon them are genuinely better off" (1990, p. 5). James Kouzes and Barry Posner talk about "how leaders get extraordinary things done in organizations" (1987, p. xv).

All these leaders emphasize *results;* they stress that successful leaders choose strategies that lead to results. If old ways of getting results fail, new ways must be tried. When BUILD's confrontational strategies alienated the business community in Baltimore, its members began to collaborate with businesspeople to address educational needs. When Denver Mayor Federico Peña's political influence was too slight to carry the physical infrastructure bond issue, he created a constituency for change by asking citizens to define needs and priorities. The purpose of collaboration, like that of any other leadership strategy, is to get results.

Achieving results is not easy. There are many obstacles to working together effectively. One significant obstacle is the perception that collaboration as a leadership strategy is fundamentally flawed. Too many people have experienced the "tyranny of consensus" in endless meetings that go nowhere. Others have been alienated when betrayed by those they had learned to trust. Task-oriented people—and this includes many business leaders—find the attention to process frustrating and want to "just do it," not recognizing that there is no power to act without the group's consent. Community people are angered by elected leaders who use collaboration for political cover for their own agendas. And for "process junkies," feeling good may take precedence over achieving results. However, when collaboration fails to lead to action and results (as it too often does), it is not because it is a poor strategy but because it is poorly executed.

Collaborative initiatives work when all of the tasks of leadership are consciously and effectively performed. They are well designed because the context is well understood. They create a constituency for change because the appropriate people are engaged in constructive ways with good information. They envision new directions, define problems, and develop solutions because participants trust each other and have skills to work together. They achieve results because members are inspired to overcome obstacles by their collective commitment. When collaborative initiatives are well executed, they achieve extraordinary results of unexpected dimensions.

The Power of Collaboration

The collaborative premise, restated, is this: if you bring the appropriate people together in constructive ways with good information, they will create authentic visions and strategies for addressing the shared concerns of the organization or community. Our study of more than fifty cases found this premise to be true. We also found that the results of collaboration went far beyond the tangible results we were looking for when we identified the exemplary cases. Those results fall generally into four categories. First, successful collaborative initiatives do achieve tangible results: problems are solved, programs are implemented, structures are changed, plans are created, roads and bridges are built. Second, these initiatives create new, unique, "virtual" processes that lead to agreement on solutions and implementable actions when nothing else is working. Third, they empower citizens and groups; participants in successful initiatives take on new and different leadership roles in their communities. Fourth (and most significant), they fundamentally change the way communities "do business" on complex issues. New collaborations on other problems are spun off. In most cases, there is no going back to older ways of doing business. In contrast to the failures of traditional politics, collaborative initiatives solve problems, bring diverse people together in constructive ways, and engage citizens on issues that affect them.

Achieving Tangible Results

The tangible results that we witnessed varied from setting a context for action to specific responses to more narrowly defined problems. In our research, three of the exemplary cases—the Newark Collaboration Group, Roanoke Vision, and the Phoenix Futures Forum—were wide-ranging efforts with an initial focus on creating a vision or broad framework for action. The framework then became the context for future decisions and actions. As the projects matured, direction became more focused, leading to the implementation of specific policies and programs. Because of the need for a broad consensus about direction, some of these efforts involved several thousand people in the community. Citizens for Denver's Future, the Baltimore Commonwealth, and the American Leadership Forum were responses to more clearly defined problems and involved fewer people because of the narrower focus.

Before the Phoenix Futures Forum (PFF) began, "business as usual" on the city's public issues meant involving the fewest people possible in decision making. This necessarily piecemeal approach could not cope with the problems caused by the massive population growth of the previous three decades. To break the deadlock, *many* citizens had to be engaged in ways that would comprehensively address the problems of growth. This was the primary objective of PFF.

The magnitude of the project challenged the policy committee's organizing and communicating skills. Four major community forums were held to bring citizens together; in addition, there were miniforums designed to reach out to the community around specific subject areas. The carefully designed forums helped participants answer questions such as, "Where are we?" and "Where do we want to go?" In one forum, for example, citizens identified a set of values to live by and created a vision statement. Eventually, thousands of people and hundreds of organizations were involved in molding a vision that would provide direction and structure for future action. After fifteen months of hard work, Phoenix had a vision statement and an implementation plan that were unanimously approved and adopted by the city council. Businessman Frank Fiore describes the vision as "something like a constitution. Here are the values we hold to be true, and here are the specific recommendations to build a society that will meet those values." PFF director and professional planner Rod Engelen says of the work done by citizens, "I think it actually worked out better than if it had been done by a bunch of professionals. It was a much, much richer flow of ideas, concerns, and needs." Now the ambitious plan had to be turned into action to take advantage of the strong constituency for change created in its development.

As the work moved from planning to action, the structure of

PFF changed to meet the changing needs. The mayor and the council appointed an Action Committee to oversee implementation for two years. Most of the committee members had participated in developing the vision and reflected the broad cross-section of stakeholders represented in that earlier phase. Their task was to take the recommendations—especially the twenty-one major initiatives requiring significant changes in policy and direction—and find champions who could move them to action. They organized themselves into six action groups to find and mobilize partners in business, government, and volunteer groups who could implement the recommendations.

Many community visioning efforts break down once the vision and strategic initiatives are identified. Alan Hald, the Action Committee chairman and vice chairman of Micro Age Inc., describes what happened after the four visioning forums were completed: "We're having difficulty shifting our gears from a planning process to an implementation process. There's lots of excitement putting ideas in. It's more difficult getting people excited about taking the actions, which implies time and energy and work commitment." Implementing organizations, particularly local governments, also get bogged down in political and turf battles that destroy the larger consensus developed in the visioning process.

Phoenix avoided these pitfalls because of the mayor's commitment to implementation. The vision and strategic initiatives were "institutionalized" through structural changes in the city council and other aspects of city government. The council set up six subcommittees to match the six action groups of PFF's Action Committee and appointed a senior member of the city manager's office to be responsible for implementation tasks assigned to city government. The city manager also set up a strategic planning organization that would work closely with the council and PFF liaison staff to ensure that the future direction of city government would be consistent with the vision. Alan Hald notes, "We are making more progress right now with the city incorporating PFF ideas than I think we are in our own internal organization implementation. The reason is that the city is organized to implement."

Collaborative initiatives elsewhere have been equally success-ful. In 1989 Denver voters passed a $242 million physical infra-structure bond package by a large margin. Today one can see the improvements paid for by the bonds all across the city. Roads are being resurfaced and bridges built. There is a new fire station. The Stock Show grounds sport some new buildings. Several parks have new facilities and rejuvenated landscapes. The county jail has a new addition. City employees finally work in air-conditioned city hall offices. The hefty bond package passed because it had the sup-port of Citizens for Denver's Future (CDF), the ninety-two-person committee that had done the hard work of making the choices about what projects would be funded.

One obstacle to CDF's success was the parochialism of Denver's different neighborhoods. Each member of CDF came from a dif-ferent neighborhood or interest group, and all had different needs. The problem was how to get people to look at what was in the best interests of the city instead of the narrow interests of their neigh-borhood or group. David Miller, one of Mayor Federico Peña's aides, attributes CDF's success partly to the open process whereby any resident could come and state his or her needs. Another suc-cess factor is the tone set by the initiative's leaders, Harry Lewis and Tim Sandos, who emphasized the need to look at projects from the perspective of the city rather than from narrower parochial views. They convinced committee members that if they could not reach a consensus, no bond issue would be likely to pass and thus nothing would happen. When the committee finished its work, it had built strong agreement about the size and composition of the package. Now it had to gain the approval of the city council.

From the beginning, CDF leaders referred to their work as cre-ating a set of recommendations for the council to act on. This non-threatening approach kept council members at bay until the recommendations were brought forward for approval. CDF co-chair Harry Lewis says, "The first dose of reality was when we ran into the council." Two council members initially refused to endorse the committee's recommendations and decided to hold their own hearings. CDF members took an active role in those hearings, at times publicly confronting the council about conflicts between items in the CDF package and those advocated by council members. As the hearings progressed, the council began to recognize the widespread public support for the CDF recommendations. Finally, the council unanimously approved a bond package virtually identical to that presented by CDF. The eventual acquiescence of the council could not have occurred without the widely publicized efforts and strong consensus of the committee.

Instituting Effective Problem-Solving Processes

In each of the exemplary cases we examined, pressing need and frustration with the ineffectiveness of other efforts led citizens and civic leaders to create new and unique processes to solve problems. They recognized that there were no experts who could solve the problems for them, no leaders with the clout to unilaterally impose solutions, and no models from other cities that could cope with their situation. With little precedent, they set out to discover or create a way of working together effectively.

The year 1986 was a turning point for the Newark Collaboration Group (NCG). The group completed "City Life," a strategic plan for the city. This plan identified strategies that would lead to the city's goals of increasing housing stock, enhancing commercial and industrial activities, creating educational and job opportunities, and improving the city's competitive position in the region. The plan guided the redevelopment of the city and suggested specific projects and programs in each of the goal areas it identified.

Before NCG was created, the city had no forum, mediating body, or leaders that could end the slow disintegration of the city and develop a consensus around a plan such as "City Life." The formation of NCG created a process and a climate wherein civic-minded citizens and leaders could come together to address the city's problems. For many participants, this result was more important than any tangible outcome. Prudential's Steven Ross notes that NCG "provided a context and a vehicle for coming together, staying together, and finding support." It established a place for dialogue between people who had positions of power and people who perceived themselves as fairly powerless. Ramon Rivera, of La Casa Don Pedro, says, "We have been brought into relationships with people we would ordinarily not have been talking to, particularly in the public sector." Trust between different races, sectors, and economic classes grew out of the safe haven provided by NCG. People could work on solutions rather than tearing each other down.

By bringing citizens together from all parts of the city, NCG established a network of people who could work together constructively and bring a common focus to the efforts of the city's various interest groups. Participants could work through strategies about what needed to happen, who needed to be involved, and what resources were necessary. It was a catalyst for bringing in organizations that could implement programs and provide leadership and administrative support. For instance, in some of NCG's housing initiatives, the group enlisted the Local Initiatives Support Corporation (LISC) to be the implementing organization while NCG provided guidance and oversight. Maria Vizcarrondo-DeSoto believes that the most important thing to remember about NCG is that "it is an ongoing, continuous process. It won't have an end for a very long time. Now there is a vehicle that's continually looking at and trying to address the issues facing the city."

The work of citizens and civic leaders through NCG also produced tangible results. Assistance was provided for developers to energize the moribund housing market, for example. One of NCG's first projects was to help Donald Harris, a gifted African-American entrepreneur, purchase land from the city to build townhouses within blocks of the site of the 1967 riots. After an agonizingly slow process to cajole the city into selling the land, Harris built forty-two new middle-income townhouses. More than a thousand additional units were added later in the same area by another developer, whose involvement was also facilitated by NCG. NCG expedited the city approval process and organized financing for both these developments when city planners and bankers had too little confidence to push investment forward.

The tangible results of collaboration in Newark went beyond housing. NCG's work in education eventually led to the formation of the Newark Education Council (NEC). Prudential's Steven Ross asserts that NEC has built a constituency for education that is much bigger than just those who control the resources: "It's engaged parents, businesspeople, university people, and teachers in policy development in ways they would not have been involved in before." The Newark Arts Council was restructured, over $2 billion was invested in downtown redevelopment, and the Newark Literacy Campaign was started. The broader vision established by "City Life" set the context for action, while NCG provided the spark for specific programs and projects.

The Baltimore Commonwealth started with the goal of keeping students in school to prepare them for jobs in business. Arnie Graf, one of the partnership's early organizers, says, "[The Baltimore Commonwealth] has the finest, most extensive, and most inclusive package of incentives for high school graduates of any in the country." Students with a 95 percent attendance record are designated Commonwealth Plus students. Upon graduation, each student is guaranteed help in entering college, three job interviews with local businesses, and (if no job is available) placement in a job training program. An operations committee within the school system is responsible for working with school-based teams to communicate and implement the Commonwealth's programs. The College Bound Foundation provides financial assistance for college to any student in Baltimore City Public Schools, and the business community contributes to that foundation's scholarship fund. Having started with incentives to keep students in school, the Commonwealth is now turning to curriculum reform, seeking to identify the competencies that graduating students need and to begin the hard work of change within the schools.

These successes would have been impossible without the focus provided by the Baltimore Commonwealth. A piecemeal approach to keeping students in school could never have had the impact of an integrated, complementary set of programs and incentives that meet the needs of many students. In fact, most of the ideas that led to the package would not have occurred without the spark created by people working with others. One person, or even a small group of people, does not have the vision or the creativity to see the possibilities that arise out of collaborative interaction. Bob Keller, the president of the Greater Baltimore Committee, says, "We're really creating a system in which change can occur." According to Linda Harris, Baltimore's director of employment development, the Commonwealth should be viewed more as a strategy for bringing all the resources together than as a simple program intervention. Mayor Kurt Schmoke describes the Commonwealth as a "unifying project for the whole city."

Empowering Citizens and Civic Leaders

The most extraordinary and unexpected result of successful collaboration is that people are empowered and energized by their engagement in collaborative projects. Participants find out experientially that they can make a difference, that they can be heard, and that a group of diverse people can constructively address complex civic issues. John Hall, a university professor in Phoenix, found that "people who got involved [in PFF activities] came away feeling they had a voice. For people who were cynical about participation, I think the evidence is clear that that can be changed through their involvement." Columnist Tom Spratt attributes the large turnout of citizens for Forum activities to the good work of the organizers in "creating a way for people to express what they thought about the problems in the city." It was a place where people felt they had some control over what was happening in the city. In Newark, notes Steven Ross, most of the results of NCG are "the products of people who are affected by, infected by, inspired by the collaboration." They work together to pursue common goals and take advantage of the receptive environment created by the collaboration to do things that could not be done before.

Citizens and civic leaders learn that they can trust others and count on their help when needed. Ross points out that "people form connections of their own around specific issues and sustain them beyond the confines of NCG." Baltimore's assistant superintendent of schools, Herman Howard, feels that the Commonwealth provides "an excellent reservoir of resources that are out there. I'll call someone, and I feel as though they're really an extension of what I'm all about and that they will provide assistance where assistance is needed." Senior Fellows of the American Leadership Forum claim that the trust and connections developed in the program have created a network that they can call on when they want to accomplish something in the community. One Fellow, an executive of a large bank, notes that the shared experience in ALF "created a base of acceptance and you jump forward from that" into other endeavors.

Empowerment is especially manifested when participants see new possibilities and roles for themselves as leaders and begin to act on those possibilities. The collaborative process helps identify potential leaders and make them more conspicuous. Rod Engelen, PFF director, speaks of a "whole new generation of leadership starting to emerge" as Forum participants from all sectors have taken major leadership roles in the community. He believes that "a whole new set of connections and leadership is probably the most important thing to come out of the Forum." Citizens for Denver's Future participant Chris Gates feels that one of the really positive outcomes of the process was that "it created some new leadership, some new candidates who had never run for office before." For example, Tim Sandos, CDF co-chair, ran for and won a city council position. Lee White, a Denver investment banker, says that Sandos's work with CDF "catapulted him onto a new plateau of political acceptability."

American Leadership Forum Fellows have created new organizations, processes, and structures to wrestle with old problems in their various cities. In one example, a white female hospital president and an African-American male activist, playwright, and poet whose sister had died of breast cancer collaborated to create a new approach to raising awareness of breast cancer in the African-American community. The norms for women in their community were fear of or lack of awareness about mammograms and hushed attitudes about cancer in general. The playwright wrote a play about his sister's death—a play that is being performed throughout the black community. The hospital's foundation sponsors the performances at community centers and schools. Medical staff attend to provide advice and to invite women to come to the hospital. One reporter says, "That's the perfect kind of collaboration that ought to come out of a program like this."

Empowerment as a result of successful engagement with others around common problems provides new insights into the nature of the term. The word as it is now used has become increasingly meaningless. People talk readily of the need to "empower" others, but no one can figure out how to do it. This research suggests some answers. When people are engaged constructively and effectively with others around issues that affect them or that they care about, they can achieve tangible results—and, in the process, they will be empowered. Efforts to empower people so that they can solve their own problems are doomed to fail. No one can "empower" others.

Instead, empowerment is something people must do for themselves. But we can engage others in collaborative approaches to solving problems of shared concern and, in the process, realize the benefits of empowerment.

Changing the Way Communities "Do Business" on Public Issues

The most important result to come out of successful collaborative initiatives is a revolutionary change in the culture of the community. New ways of leading and creating change are learned. As initiative follows initiative, an irreversible change occurs. Doors to participation are opened. Citizens successfully engaged in collaboratively addressing public problems begin to *expect* to be involved. New and different stakeholders brought to the table can no longer be excluded from future initiatives. Participants in successful efforts spin off new collaborative initiatives on other issues. Communities learn a new way of "doing business" around public concerns. Advocacy changes to engagement, hostility to civility, confrontation to conversation, and separation to community. A new civic culture is created.

For example, American Leadership Forum Fellows in Hartford served as a catalyst to bring a community-wide perspective to pediatric health care in their region. In past years, local hospitals had competed for resources to build increasingly technologically advanced treatment facilities. Under the old scheme, corporate leaders were recruited to head fund-raising drives and new hospitals were built with little knowledge or concern about the community's needs. Success was measured in terms of money raised and technological advancement, not responsiveness to needs.

In 1989 one Hartford hospital proposed to build a new comprehensive children's hospital, and as one hospital board member puts it, "All hell broke loose." The city's other hospitals immediately raised objections, and useful discussion ceased. A turf war began—and with it, an expensive campaign (about $1 million was spent) to convince the State Commission on Hospitals and Health Care to approve or reject the proposal. No one was pleased with the tone of the campaign and the lack of constructive discussion.

To break the impasse and develop a broader, more objective view of Hartford's pediatric health-care needs, ALF Fellows convened a meeting of the major players in the health-care system, including members of the community and business representatives, to review the purpose of the new proposal. The highly charged meeting stopped business as usual and led to a deeper exploration of Hartford's needs. A nationally known hospital consulting group was retained to conduct a major study. The results of the study pointed to a great need for preventive services coupled with a new, appropriately sized, fiscally sound children's hospital. It also suggested that government, business, and health-care leaders put aside their rivalries and seize the opportunity to meet the city's pediatric health-care needs in more constructive ways.

The intervention of the ALF Fellows has changed the way Hartford now deals with pediatric health-care concerns. One result was the founding of the Child Council in the summer of 1991. That organization's mission is to improve medical care for the city's poorest children. More than thirty leaders—health-care and social service professionals, representatives of African-American and Hispanic groups, educators, and citizens—come together on an ongoing basis to assess what medical needs they want to tackle and how to go about doing it. The Council parcels out funds from a newly established foundation to programs and initiatives that clearly help address the needs of the community. The role of corporations has changed too; they no longer blindly support fund-raising for new hospitals without understanding the broader needs of the community.

Citizens in several other projects have observed similar shifts in approaches to public issues. Harry Lewis of Denver says, "I think the day of the strong mayor approach, where former Mayor McNichols came out of a smoke-filled room and called for a bond election overnight, is over." Phoenix businessman Alan Hald notes, "The key thing we're doing is changing the nature of governance. Traditionally, governance has been dependent on what government does. Now we're saying it's really dependent on how citizens, the private sector, community-based organizations, and government work together to effect change." Dr. Stanley Bergen believes that "the Newark Collaboration Group has reassured people that a collaborative process can take the place of a confrontational process and that you don't have to take to the streets, burn down buildings, and lock people in." Alex Plinio, the Prudential executive who started NCG, describes that organization's impact on Newark in this way: "Openness, bringing people to the table, consensus, and better communication are more highly valued now by those who want to get things done." When collaboration works, there is no going back to older ways of doing business. The door opened by inclusion and engagement of citizens in public issues can no longer be closed.

From Vision to Action

The accomplishments of collaboration do not come without effort. They arise out of careful attention to the tasks of leadership: understanding the context for collaboration, creating a constituency for change, setting direction, and getting results. Each task depends on the execution of the previous task for success. Getting results means a shift in attention from vision to action.

Getting results is too often where collaborative efforts fail. Agreements reached about vision, problem definition, and solutions are not followed by well-organized, well-managed approaches to implementation and action. There must be a clear shift from a focus on planning to a focus on getting results. Some structure for managing and evaluating implementation needs to be created. Participants must create an action plan and find the leadership to turn collaborative agreements into action.

Many collaborative initiatives set up a separate structure to manage and provide oversight for implementation. The Phoenix Futures Forum established an Action Committee to guide the six action groups responsible for implementing the twenty-one action strategies. These "steering" groups are responsible for creating a detailed plan or process design for moving each strategy into action. The end result is a clear definition of roles, responsibilities, and timelines that will lead to action.

Sometimes collaborative agreements about vision or strategic goals remain so complex that other, smaller-scale collaborative initiatives must be set up to further refine problem definition, develop specific solutions, and gain the "ownership" of those who must implement the plan. The Atlanta Regional Commission (ARC) recently guided citizens in the Atlanta, Georgia, region through an extensive public visioning process. The resulting plan, Vision 20/20, identifies broad strategic goals in such areas as education, transportation, and health care. ARC then brought together more than 100 citizens in the region to develop interventions that would lead to action for each of the strategic goals. The role of these leaders is to serve as conveners and catalysts to get the right people together and help them reach agreements about necessary actions that are consistent with the vision. Their tasks are to find leaders who will champion both these new goals and the organizations that must do the work and then to create a team with the capacity and commitment to sustain action.

Collaborative initiatives get results because participants take deliberate actions to achieve them. Here are some examples of specific actions we identified that helped produce results in the groups we studied:

- Consciously shifting focus from planning to results
- Establishing a management structure and review process to oversee implementation
- Establishing detailed action plans for each implementation initiative that include clear timelines and assignments of roles and responsibilities
- Finding champions and creating implementation teams with the capacity and commitment to initiate and sustain action
- "Spinning off" implementation tasks to existing organizations (or creating new ones, if necessary)
- Securing agreement of implementing organizations to goals, strategies, and implementation tasks

The results of collaboration are far-reaching. Successful efforts produce tangible results, empower participants, lead to revolutionary changes in civic culture, and create a renewed, deeper sense of community. Empowerment and community are created when these successful efforts engage citizens constructively to address issues and problems they care about. These results do not come about through interventions or activities designed solely to empower or create community. Engagement on real issues is the key.

Part Three

New Visions of Leadership and Civic Action

In successful collaborative initiatives, leadership is focused primarily on the success of the collective endeavor. Differences in power and authority among participants are almost ignored. What emerges is a pattern of behavior analogous to what others have called *transforming, servant,* or *facilitative* leadership. This kind of leadership is characterized by its focus on promoting and safeguarding the process (rather than on individual leaders taking decisive action). While this kind of leadership is different than that traditionally practiced, it is clear from participants that the necessary leadership capacities can be acquired or enhanced through systematic development.

A deep, profound response to the failure of traditional politics is occurring in America's cities and regions. Citizens and civic leaders alike are acting with increasing confidence, taking on the problems of their communities in collaborative ways. They are bringing together elected leaders, old line civic leaders, and influential people along with citizens who previously found few avenues for effective participation in civic affairs. Their purpose is to discover new approaches for engaging on public issues that break gridlock and heal the divisions of the community. These collaborative practices are deeply democratic and effective; they get results, empower citizens, renew a sense of community, and build a new civic culture.

Chapter Eight

Skills for a New Kind of Leadership

The role of leadership in collaboration is to engage others by designing constructive processes for working together, convene appropriate stakeholders, and facilitate and sustain their interaction. In this different kind of leadership, leaders promote and safeguard the collaborative process rather than take unilateral, decisive action. The power of position is of little help in this world of peers, nor are the traditional hierarchical, political, and confrontational models of leadership. Those who lead collaborative efforts—transforming, facilitative, "servant" leaders—rely on both a new vision of leadership and new skills and behaviors to help communities and organizations realize their visions, solve problems, and get results.

The Basic Leadership Types

Leadership is exercised in an endless variety of contexts. For us to better understand leadership in the emerging context of collaboration, we need to see how collaborative leadership compares with the two predominant forms of leadership in our culture, tactical leadership and positional leadership.

Tactical Leadership

Tactical leadership (sometimes referred to as heroic leadership) is exercised when the objective is very clear—win the game, defeat the enemy, remove the cancerous tumor, apprehend the suspect— a plan for achieving the objective has been developed, and the members of the collective effort are being led in the execution of that plan. Military commanders, coaches, surgeons, commanders of law enforcement tactical teams (SWAT and SCAT teams, for example), and directors of film and theater productions are just a few of the many tactical leaders we can enumerate.

Many of our notions about leadership come from the tactical situation—in fact, many of us had our own early experiences with leadership in that arena—and our heroes are often tactical leaders. But leadership in tactical situations, though extremely widespread, is nevertheless unique. The tactical leader clarifies the goal, convinces us that it is absolutely essential to achieve that goal, explains the plan and strategies, organizes and coordinates our activities, and deals aggressively with individual performance issues.

Positional Leadership

Positional leadership is associated with being at the top of a functional structure. For many people, including the media, *leadership* and *position* are synonymous. It is the second context within which most of us have experience that has shaped our notions of leadership.

The CEO of a corporation, the head librarian, the supervisor of a construction crew, the dean of a college, the curator of a museum, the manager of a restaurant, and "my boss" are positional leaders. The positional leader is in charge of a structure (a unit or an entire organization) whose purpose is to perform a set of tasks or activities. Like the tactical leader, the positional leader sets goals, organizes activities, motivates and rewards, and so on. And like tactical leaders, positional leaders are often well known and well paid, and they are even sometimes idolized.

These two dominant forms of leadership are well established in our culture. When enacted well, they inspire and energize us. Successful tactical and positional leaders are celebrated in novels and movies, occasionally even songs. They are critical to a great many worthwhile and noble endeavors. But neither tactical nor positional leadership works in the collaborative context.

Collaborative Leadership

In our research on successful collaboration, we found another form of leadership characterized by very different roles and tasks. There are several reasons why these different roles and tasks emerged. First, collaborative efforts cross many boundaries. Participants come from the public and private sectors and from the broader community. They are not members of a single organization but rather come from many different organizations and institutions. Their training, experiences, and values differ markedly. There are many different values—religious, educational, political, industrial, and so on—represented in the group. The typical tactical or positional leader deals with a much more homogeneous "follower" group. A football coach, a military commander, a symphony conductor, a senior vice president of marketing, or a corporate CEO is likely to interact with a much less diverse group of people than someone who initiates a community collaboration. Collaborative leaders usually have no formal power or authority. They exercise leadership in what is perhaps the most difficult context—when all are peers. To assume that participants in a collaborative initiative will accept tactical or positional leadership is a mistake. The application of these forms of leadership to collaborative endeavors usually leads to failure.

Second, strategies for getting results in situations demanding collaboration are unclear even though problems may be clearly evident. The city is experiencing runaway growth and development. The students are dropping out of public school at an alarming rate. The physical infrastructure of the city is deteriorating. Gang violence has escalated to the point where residents of the community fear for their safety. These are urgent problems, but they are so complex that there is little agreement about how to proceed. These are not tactical issues like achieving increased quarterly earning statements for shareholders or winning the championship. These are not routine challenges. There is no agreement on the problems themselves, on possible solutions, or even on how to move ahead.

Third, leadership in collaborative initiatives does not rely on content or subject-matter expertise as it does in tactical or positional leadership approaches. The coach knows the game and has studied the opposition. The CEO knows his or her organization and the market. Military commanders know military tactics and have intelligence at their disposal to make decisions. Collaborative leaders have a different focus—promoting and safeguarding the collaborative process. They rely on the group to work with the content and substance of the issues. Their task is to see to it that the process is constructive and leads to results, not to impose their own answers to collective issues. The questions they face have only the answers the group can agree upon. What do we want the future of our city to be? How can we create and put into place a strengthened network of community leaders? What will keep the kids from dropping out of school? There are no given answers to these questions. The answers must emerge from the interaction of the stakeholders. The formation of the Newark Collaboration Group and its impact on the revitalization of the city provides a striking example of collaborative leadership in action.

Collaborative Leadership in Newark, New Jersey

The kind of leadership that began to rebuild the decaying physical, social, and financial foundations of Newark was fundamentally different from tactical or positional leadership. Whereas in other cities facing similar conditions experts and governments had been immobilized by their inability to solve their problems, Newark's civic leaders recognized that citizens would have to do the hard work of defining problems, establishing a vision, and creating strategies that would counter the city's slow disintegration.

In 1967 Newark suffered through five days and nights of riots after two white police officers allegedly beat a black taxi driver. Twenty-six people were killed and more than a thousand were injured as houses and businesses were looted and burned. With much of the city scorched and ruined, Newark reminded many of a war zone. "It was ugly; . . . it looked like a bombed-out city," recalls Monsignor Franklyn Casale of the Archdiocese. In the aftermath of the riots, few people held much hope for Newark's future. In a shock wave of violence and destruction, Newark seemed fated to become a permanent symbol of urban decay, neglect, and poverty in America.

For fifteen years after 1967, the city continued its downward spiral as more than 25 percent of the city's population, mostly middle-class whites, fled to safer suburbs. The poorer inner-city residents who remained had to rebuild their lives, homes, and neighborhoods as best they could. By 1980 the population of the city consisted of more than 80 percent minorities: two-thirds African-Americans, one-third Hispanics, and a smattering of Asians. Crime rates rose dramatically as an urban drug culture flourished. Housing continued to deteriorate, and businesses left the inner city in droves. Without a single supermarket left, residents of the hardest hit Central Ward had to travel to adjoining neighborhoods to buy groceries. Racial tension increased as the economic divisions between poor minorities and wealthier whites grew. Federal resources to benefit cities were dramatically reduced by the Reagan Administration's new federalism, which turned much of the responsibility for urban renewal over to cities and states.

The city had gone through a "wrenching change," says Stanley Bergen, president of the University of Medicine and Dentistry of New Jersey: "A mayor went to jail, ethnic fragmentation, serious problems with crime, and large population loss." These changes left the city bereft of any sense of shared concern for the future. Over the years, several groups attempted to revitalize Newark, but their efforts were so fragmented they never made a real difference. Black political leaders and white business leaders competed for development resources, polarizing the city's leadership. Leaders of nonprofit organizations and neighborhood groups squabbled over turf issues. Distrustful and wary, Newark's fragmented leadership fought to protect parochial interests. Nationally, the city's reputation as a symbol of urban decay continued to fester. Saul Fenster, of the New Jersey Institute of Technology, remarks pointedly, "It's really hard to find a city that has had to deal with this burden of reputation."

In 1984 things began to change. For several years prior to this, rumors circulated that Prudential, an insurance company and one of the city's largest employers, would abandon the city as economic and social conditions deteriorated. Instead of leaving the city, however, the company decided in 1984 to expand its headquarters and to encourage other major corporations to stay. This decision was pivotal in Newark's renewal. "Prudential provided a sense of confidence," says Norman Samuels, provost of Rutgers's Newark campus. It was part of an economic base that enabled the city to survive hard times. More important, the corporation decided to take a strong leadership role in addressing the pressing needs of the city.

Prudential, strongly affected by the city's tarnished image, had its own reasons for acting. Employee safety, housing, and education were serious concerns as the city's quality of life and ability to deliver services declined through the 1970s. Realizing that its success was directly tied to the success of the city, the company assigned Alex Plinio to a new position in public affairs, giving him responsibility for managing its civic activities. Plinio saw many problems confronting Newark. At the beginning of his assignment, he recalls, "There was no major move in the city to attempt to comprehensively address these problems." He wanted to find out what the company could do to help the city.

Over the next several months, Plinio interviewed over fifty of the city's top leaders, including presidents of universities, city council members, heads of corporations, heads of community groups, directors of drug rehabilitation centers, and others. Plinio "wanted to determine whether or not there was enough leadership to address the major issues and to find out if people would be willing to work together."

At the same time, his staff began to investigate how other cities had worked together to solve common problems. One clear lesson emerged: most city partnerships were between government and business and excluded community groups, nonprofits, educational representatives, and other key stakeholders. In many cases, these excluded groups were able to block initiatives of the "public/private" partnerships. By leaving out key perspectives and interests, the authors of these initiatives were unable to create a powerful enough constituency to implement their recommendations. Plinio wanted to create a collaborative approach that would include all the city's stakeholders.

Plinio was able to convince Prudential's president, David Sherwood, to support a community-wide collaborative effort with a financial contribution from the company and with the president's personal participation. Recognizing the need to involve as many of the city's high-level leaders as possible, Plinio had Sherwood and five other top leaders, including the mayor, Ken Gibson, invite thirty-five other leaders from throughout the city to an initial meeting. "We had the core of the city there," says Plinio. "The meeting had a very simple agenda. We asked a couple of questions: What's good about Newark? What's bad about Newark? What, if anything, do you want to do about either of these things?" Plinio wanted to find out if people cared enough to work together to improve the city. The meeting also created an opportunity for leaders to come together who were often in conflict with each other or did not know one another, and Plinio secured their agreement to work together in subsequent sessions.

David Straus, one of the pioneers in designing and facilitating community-wide collaborative initiatives, facilitated these first meetings of what would become the Newark Collaboration Group (NCG). Straus, the co-founder of the collaborative consulting firm Interaction Associates, Inc., played a key role in NCG's early success. He helped the group learn how to work by consensus. Ramon Rivera of La Casa Don Pedro notes that "the process laid out some guidelines that we all agreed to. One of these was to use consensus and be inclusive. That means everyone was allowed to be a part of it." He pointed out one especially important aspect of the process: "Not only were we zeroing in on our own agendas; we were also looking at other people's input and their particular agendas." Cathy McFarland of the Victoria Foundation recalls that "it was mostly talking and listening—listening to others. People were getting to know each other. People still had their own agendas, but they were willing to buy into the whole agenda because they saw that that was how they'd be able to achieve their agenda." The relationships, structure, and common agenda that evolved out of these first meetings provided the foundations for NCG's later success.

By 1985 NCG's work began to focus more on substance than on building relationships and identifying common concerns. Its mission was now clear: NCG would work toward redeveloping Newark, increasing the housing stock, enhancing commercial and industrial activities, creating educational and job opportunities for Newark's residents, and improving the city's competitive position in the region. A strategic plan would be developed to identify strategies and resources for addressing these needs. Steven Ross, another Prudential executive, says, "NCG would identify initiatives and the people or organizations that could move them forward." NCG was "never intended to take on municipal responsibilities, to replace the functions of government." NCG's role was to convene civic leaders and citizens and to help facilitate actions that no one group or sector could accomplish alone.

As the strategic plan, known as "City Life," evolved, several key factors contributed to its success. Participants in NCG regularly sought the input of the broader community and of leaders and organizations that would have to implement its recommendations. The plan stated that "there would be early 'buy-in' by key interests to assure that decision makers accepted the process and could commit themselves to seeing it successfully accomplished." Steven Ross says that "participants wouldn't consider the plan complete until it identified not only how things would get done but by whom." In order to gain support for implementation, the process had to maintain its focus on inclusion, openness, and consensus.

Parallel tracks were created to provide opportunities for short-term successes while the longer-term goals were being developed. This allowed the group, in Steven Ross's words, "to demonstrate some competence" and learn how to actually do something. The bringing together of different perspectives and interests sparked a number of creative activities that simply would not have occurred without the structure of NCG. George Hampton, of the University of Medicine and Dentistry of New Jersey, says, "People were willing to look beyond their own turf boundaries, beyond their own selfish needs, to the greater good of the entire city." By learning to trust one another, gaining the commitment of high-level leaders, working together in a carefully facilitated way, including stakeholders from throughout the community, seeking consensus, and taking small, achievable steps, participants in NCG began to break the gridlock of previous years.

The first signs of success appeared in 1985 with an increase in real estate development. Newark, a *New York Times* article reported, had benefited from New York City's exorbitant real estate prices, but some of the progress was attributed to Newark citizens' efforts to "help themselves." An urban specialist from Rutgers, quoted by the paper, said Newark was changing because of "a core of people who are working hard and meeting regularly, coming up with ideas and plans" (Perlez, 1985, p. E6). The specialist specifically pointed to the efforts of the Newark Collaboration Group. In 1986, a *New York Times* editorial said, in praising the strategic plan, that the "sober contributions of civic benefactors like the Newark Collaboration Group" would be indispensable in preparing the city for the twenty-first century ("Next Century Newark," 1986, p. 26). Newark was learning to work together not just within isolated neighborhoods or sectors but throughout the city. It had created a forum in which problems of shared concern could be addressed. It was a long-awaited beginning to the city's renewal—a renewal from within that relied not on outsiders or government but on the care and commitment of its citizens.

Since the early 1980s, Newark has made remarkable progress. More than 7,500 units of housing have been built or rehabilitated, with 1,100 of these units sponsored by community organizations and nonprofits. One-third of these units are intended for low-income residents. The city has developed one of the most successful urban recycling programs in the world, with over 60 percent of its garbage recycled. (The program was implemented as part of a massive neighborhood cleanup effort and has saved the city several million dollars in disposal costs.) More than $2 billion has been invested in office, commercial, and industrial development in downtown in recent years. Community organizations such as the New Community Corporation (NCC) have been instrumental in helping to address the most serious problems in the devastated Central Ward with programs for housing, child care, health services, education, and employment and job services. NCC's founder, Monsignor William Lindner, put together $16 million in state and federal grants and loans from Prudential and First Fidelity to build the neighborhood's first supermarket in twenty-three years. The market provides more than 300 jobs and accessible shopping for area residents. Two-thirds of its profits are reinvested in other community projects.

In 1991 the city received the National Civic League's (NCL) coveted All-America City Award for its collaborative revitalization efforts. The program's director, Betsy Horsley, says, "NCL was not looking to commend perfect communities. We were looking to honor those that are working hardest to solve their problems" (Underdue, 1991, p. N1). The mayor, Sharpe James, adds that the city won the award because "we chose to face our problems," not because it was perfect. In the same year, the United States Conference of Mayors awarded Newark first place in its most-livable-cities competition. Kay Scrimger, a conference spokesperson, notes that Newark was chosen "not for its intrinsic livability but for purposeful actions . . . that promote livability" (Barron, 1991, p. B1). To round out the 1991 awards, Monsignor Lindner, NCC's tireless executive director, received a John D. and Catherine T. MacArthur Foundation "genius award." And there are other measures of Newark's progress: a U.S. Environmental Protection Agency commendation of the city for its recycling efforts, the city's improved bond ratings, and the Department of Housing and Urban Development's refusal to put the Newark Housing Authority into receivership because of "emerging signs of cooperative effort" (Nieves, 1992, p. 28). "Mayor James," writes the *Christian Science Monitor*, "sees a certain poetic justice in the fact that his city, once 'kicked, stepped on, and laughed at,' is now an award winner" (Mouat, 1991, p. 8).

"Futurists have a tantalizing way of describing the year 2001 as though being there has little to do with getting there. The future simply arrives full-blown. But it is the succession of days and years between now and then that will determine what life will be like—and what we will do with each of those days and years," remarks educator John Goodlad (1990, p. 377). Newark's progress is hard-won; the result of hard work, of the invention of new ways of working together, and of sustained commitment. After years of urban stagnation, Newark's citizens have recognized that one group fighting for dominance over another will never bring renewal. Energized by the leadership of Alex Plinio, Sharpe James, William Lindner, and many others, the people of Newark are working together to address the city's needs. The Newark Collaboration Group provides a forum in which stakeholders from throughout the community can work together and have an equal voice in decisions. The New Community Corporation brings hope and real results to the most troubled neighborhoods. The commitment of Prudential and other corporations to stay and invest in the city's future offers confidence and employment opportunities.

"The secret to Newark is [that] many years of public investment are now yielding a harvest," notes Mitchell Moss of the Urban Research Center and New York University. Newark's citizens, unwilling to be overwhelmed by the enormity of the city's problems, have filled the days and years since the early 1980s with steady, cooperative efforts and are finally reaping the harvest. Mayor James concludes that "to be a senior city and be recognized for our progress, I think, is the most important message you can send. The test of Newark is the test of America. Can (older) urban centers survive and grow?" (Mouat, 1991, p. 8).

The Principles of Collaborative Leadership

The primary role of collaborative leaders is to promote and safeguard the process. All of the fifty-two successful collaborative initiatives we investigated had strong process leadership. What emerged was a pattern of behavior analogous to what others have called *transforming, servant,* or *facilitative* leadership. Four principles characterize this collaborative leadership. We will now look at each in turn.

Inspire Commitment and Action

Somebody has to do something. As Warren Bennis and Burt Nanus (1985) found in their study of a diverse sample of leaders, leadership implies a bias for action, for getting results. What makes collaborative leaders unique is that they catalyze, convene, energize, and facilitate others to create visions and solve problems. They create new alliances, partnerships, and forums. Even if they come from established *positions* of leadership, they rely on different *practices* of leadership. They lead in unfamiliar territory where few established working relationships exist. They are often met with cynicism and helplessness, both from those who consider *any* leadership activity a waste of time and from those who are accustomed to traditional leadership: "It's always been this way; it's always going to be this way; and there's nothing you can do about it." Appearances to the contrary, collaborative leaders are action-oriented. But the action involves convincing people that something can be done, not telling them what to do or doing the work for them.

Collaborative leaders bring people to the table, help them work together constructively, and keep them at the table. They do this in many different ways. In Phoenix, it was the mayor and the city planning director—both holding positions of traditional authority—who convened the citizens of Phoenix and its surrounding communities to address the city's future in the Phoenix Futures Forum. In Newark, the initial convener was acting both as a private citizen and corporate executive; the stakeholders were influential leaders and ordinary citizens from every sector of the city. The Baltimore Commonwealth was sparked by black citizens organizing around their community's concerns.

Power and influence help, but they are not the distinguishing features of collaborative leaders. The distinguishing feature is that these leaders initiate a process that brings people together when nothing else is working. (In Chapter Five, we described how they initiate the process.)

Lead as Peer Problem Solver

Collaborative leaders help groups create visions and solve problems. They do not do the work of the group for the group. They do not engage in command-and-control behavior. Who is in charge is not as important as the confidence of the stakeholders in the credibility and effectiveness of the process. Ownership of the process is shared. Power and status differences among the participants is deemphasized, and leaders engage in helping peers solve problems. Effective leadership in a world of peers may be the most difficult of all leadership roles.

Collaborative leaders must be active and involved. Their energy is invested in the people—building relationships and the process. Promoting commitment and involvement by the participants, creating a credible, open process in which participants have confidence, resisting shortcuts, protecting the process against vested interests—these are all tasks for collaborative leaders. Their role is to serve the group and the broader purpose for which it exists. Without the power of position, collaborative leaders rely instead on their credibility, integrity, and ability to focus on the process.

Build Broad-Based Involvement

Collaboration would not be as difficult as it is if it involved only those with similar beliefs and values. But its purpose is to include the relevant community of interests regardless of diversity. In complex situations, there would be no results without broad-based involvement. It is collaborative leaders who must take responsibility for building broad-based involvement. They make a conscious and disciplined effort to identify and bring together stakeholders who are necessary to define problems, create solutions, and get results. Their bias is to include more people rather than fewer. They take great pains to be inclusive, recognizing that many collaborative initiatives fail because the right people were not included.

Sustain Hope and Participation

When the inevitable frustrations and difficulties occur, collaborative leaders stand out. They convince participants that each person's input is valued. They help set incremental and obtainable goals and encourage celebrations of achievement along the way. They sustain confidence by promoting and protecting a process in which participants believe. They sustain commitment to the process at times when quick solutions are offered or when power and influence assert themselves. They keep people at the table when more traditional but destructive ways of doing business seem tempting. Collaborative leaders help groups do hard work when it would be easier to quit.

These four principles that characterize collaborative leadership require leaders to drop their concern for a particular content outcome and rely on the group. When this is not possible for someone, other individuals may need to step into the role. Tactical or positional leadership simply will not work. Someone has to attend to the roles and tasks of collaborative leadership for collaboration to succeed.

Despite our history of tactical and positional leadership approaches, collaborative leadership can be learned. The American Leadership Forum has taken several hundred leaders from all parts of the community, most with strong biases toward more traditional leadership approaches, and helped them learn how to play new roles. ALF Fellows learn the skills and attitudes associated with collaborative leadership: they learn how to convene stakeholders, promote shared responsibility and action, facilitate meetings, and create shared visions. Many of the participants in ALF classes note significant changes in their leadership attitudes and skills.

Collaborative Leadership in Theory and Practice

We have said that collaborative leadership is based on a new vision of leadership, but it shares several key ideas with the work of other leadership theorists and writers.

Transforming Leadership

James MacGregor Burns introduced the term *transforming leadership* in 1978: "The transforming leader looks for potential motives in followers, seeks to satisfy higher needs, and engages the full person" (1978, p. 4). He contrasted this form of leadership with *transactional leadership*, which involves exchanging one thing for another (and characterizes most leader/follower relationships). His ideas about transforming leadership significantly raised the stakes for what leadership should be about. He added an ethical dimension by expecting the interaction of leaders and followers to meet the needs of both while raising (transforming) each other to "higher levels of motivation and morality" (p. 20). Leaders and followers, in his mind, are peers. They simply play different roles.

The results of effective collaborative leadership are similar to those of transforming leadership. The needs of both leaders and followers are met. Stakeholders work together as peers. The whole person is engaged on issues he or she cares about. And when collaboration is successful, participants are empowered and a new sense of efficacy and community emerges—a higher level of motivation and morality. Stakeholders and communities are "transformed."

Servant Leadership

"[People] will freely respond only to individuals who are chosen as leaders because they are proven and trusted as servants," writes Robert Greenleaf in *Servant Leadership* (1977, p. 10). Like Burns, Greenleaf wants leaders to make sure others' needs are met and that they grow as persons. He asks leaders to look out for the broader needs of society. He suggests that leaders must listen and perhaps even withdraw in order to understand a situation and intervene appropriately. Servant leadership requires acceptance of others as peers. Greenleaf views the central ethic of leadership as foresight— the ability to see how things might be in the future and to act now to move in that direction. A significant purpose of servant leadership is to learn how to live in community.

Collaborative leadership as we have described it shares much with Greenleaf's ideas. Someone has to have the foresight to see another way of moving forward—a way that meets the needs of all stakeholders while accepting them as peers. Successful collaboration meets the broader needs of society and begins to teach the meaning of community. Stakeholders respond only to those collaborative leaders who have the credibility and integrity to serve the process. Collaborative leaders are servants of the group, helping stakeholders do their work.

Leadership as a Process

From John Kotter's perspective, leadership, unlike management, does not produce consistency and order; it produces movement or change—constructive or adaptive change (1990, pp. 4–5). Leadership creates change through the processes of establishing direction through vision and strategy, aligning people whose cooperation is needed to achieve the vision, and motivating and inspiring them to overcome barriers to change.

These dimensions of leadership are recurring themes in leadership studies. But Kotter pushes them in new and different directions, taking them beyond the traditional tactical and positional approaches in which the leader sets direction, aligns people by organizing them in hierarchies, and motivates (not necessarily inspires) them through incentives and power wielding. For instance, he finds that in complex organizational situations, many people are part of the overall leadership process. The problems and issues are so complex that one person cannot supply the necessary leadership to get results. "Leadership in a modest sense—i.e., leadership with a lower-case (little) 'l,'" he says, "is far more prevalent and far more important than most people realize. Not flashy or dramatic, it rarely attracts much attention and often goes unnoticed" (p. 83). He notes, too, that the structures that link both leaders and followers together are what he calls "thick, informal networks," not hierarchies (p. 89). What is needed, he says, "are good working relationships among many people" in order to establish direction, align people, and inspire them to act (p. 91).

Collaborative leadership uses similar processes to create useful change. Direction is established through the collaborative interaction of the stakeholders. Alignment occurs by building broad-based involvement (thick, informal networks) through agreements about how to work together. Motivation and inspiration happen through belief in the credibility of the collaborative process and good working relationships with many people. Collaborative leaders are rarely dramatic or flashy, and the leadership function is often shared among several people. Their role is to facilitate the constructive interaction of the network, not to do the work for it. An effective combination of these approaches creates a constituency for change that produces tangible results, empowers participants, and builds community.

How to Get Extraordinary Things Done

The book jacket for *The Leadership Challenge*, by James M. Kouzes and Barry Z. Posner (1987), describes the book as showing "that leadership is not the private preserve of a few charismatic men and women, but a learnable set of practices that virtually anyone can master." These practices, distilled from more than 500 reports of "personal bests" by private-sector leaders, suggested to Kouzes and Posner five principles for getting "extraordinary things done in organizations."

First, effective leaders *challenge the process*. They take risks, challenge the system, and challenge the way things are normally done. They experiment, innovate, and learn. They are not satisfied with the status quo.

Second, these leaders *inspire a shared vision*. "They breathe life into what are the hopes and dreams of others and enable them to see the exciting possibilities that the future holds. Leaders get others to buy into their dreams by showing how all will be served by a common purpose" (p. 10). They understand people's needs and have their interests at heart.

Third, leaders who get extraordinary things done *enable others to act*. They enlist the support of all those who are necessary to get results, as well as those who will be affected by the results. Their role is to encourage collaboration and teamwork and "make it possible for others to do good work" (p. 10). Kouzes and Posner have "developed a simple one-word test to detect whether someone is on the road to becoming a leader. That word is *we*" (p. 10).

Fourth, good leaders *model the way;* they lead by example. Their behaviors, attitudes, and actions are congruent with their stated beliefs and purposes. They are clear about their beliefs and understand that respect is earned by acting consistently with these beliefs. They practice what they preach.

Fifth, these leaders *encourage the heart.* "The climb to the top is arduous and long. People become exhausted, frustrated, and disenchanted. They often are tempted to give up. Leaders must encourage the heart of their followers to carry on" (p. 12). They understand what it takes to sustain commitment and action. They convince others that success is possible.

Collaborative leadership gets extraordinary things done in communities through similar practices. Collaborative leaders challenge the way things are being done by bringing new approaches to complex public issues when nothing else is working. They convince others that something can be done by working together. They inspire collaborative action that leads to shared vision. They empower people by engaging them on issues of shared concern and helping them achieve results by working together constructively. Their credibility comes from the congruence of their beliefs with their actions. If they espouse collaboration, they collaborate themselves. They recognize that their ability to get things done must come from respect, since they have no formal authority. They keep people at the table through difficult and frustrating times by reminding them of the common purpose and of the difficulties of achieving results with other approaches. They "encourage the heart" by helping to create and celebrate successes along the way to sustain hope and participation.

What Collaborative Leaders Do

The principles of collaborative leadership that emerged from our research are consistent with these other recent perspectives on leadership, as we have shown. The roles and practices of leadership in all of these models are defined very differently than those of the tactical and positional models of leadership. Although collaborative leaders perform similar tasks—establishing direction, aligning people in support of it, and motivating and inspiring them to achieve it—they lead in very different ways. Collaborative leaders are decidedly visionary—but about how people can work together constructively rather than about a particular vision or solution for a specific issue. These leaders transform communities in ways that achieve tangible results and, more important, change the way the community addresses complex public concerns. When these leaders engage people constructively and "model the way," people are empowered; the citizens'—and the leaders'—needs are met. A deeper sense of connectedness and community grows out of the interaction.

Collaborative leaders are sustained by their deeply democratic belief that people have the capacity to create their own visions and solve their own problems. If you can bring the appropriate people together (being broadly inclusive) in constructive ways (creating a credible, open process) with good information (bringing about a shared understanding of problems and concerns), they will create authentic visions and strategies for addressing the shared concerns of the organization or community. The leadership role is to convene, energize, facilitate, and sustain this process. As we have said, *the only consensus that really matters is that of the people who live there.*

Chapter Nine

A New Vision of Civic Action

The exemplary cases of collaboration profiled in this book demonstrate that a new kind of civic politics is arising in America's communities and regions. The approach in each place uniquely responds to the issues at hand yet holds to the principles and premises of successful collaboration that we have shared in this book. And new examples of collaboration continue to emerge in very different situations and arenas. Each one emphasizes the capacity and commitment of citizens and civic leaders to create useful change through working together in their communities and regions. As with our exemplary cases, each one was started because other approaches were not working.

But deeper motivations are beginning to emerge. Some of the initiatives are being designed not simply to solve problems but to create a new civic culture and a renewal of community. Here citizens and civic leaders recognize that the success of their communities and regions depends much more on the engagement of citizens in public affairs than on the quality of governments and elected leaders. Listen to Mayor Daniel Kemmis of Missoula, Montana: "Strong democratic instincts would inform that there will not be any salvation of politics from the direction of virtuous candidates or leaders, but that it is only through the virtue of citizenship that politics can be redeemed. . . . It will be what *we* make of it" (1992, p. 23). Americans are creating a new vision of civic action and community.

New Examples of Civic Action

In his book *What Are People For?* essayist Wendell Berry writes, "[The revival of community] would have to be a revival accomplished mainly by the community itself. It would have to be done

147

not from the outside by the instruction of visiting experts, but from the inside by the ancient rule of neighborliness, by the love of precious things, and by the wish to be at home" (1990, p. 169). Throughout this country, new examples of civic politics are arising that share this understanding. In unexpected places with very different circumstances, citizens are using collaborative approaches to resolve environmental and land-use disputes, address ethical issues, make laws in state legislatures, change the structure and practice of school governance, and cope with the challenges of urban revitalization.

Developing Bioregional Citizenship in California and Montana

Poet and essayist Gary Snyder suggests another way of understanding the word *wild* when applied to societies. The *Oxford English Dictionary* defines "wild societies" as those that are uncivilized, rude, and resisting constituted government. Snyder defines them differently: wild societies are those whose order has grown from within, whose order is maintained by the force of consensus and custom rather than explicit legislation, and that have an economic system that is in a close and sustainable relation to the local ecosystem (1990, p. 10). Snyder sees as necessary the congruence of the needs of the land with the needs of human beings. To sustain themselves, wild societies depend on a deep communal connection between each member of society and with the land.

The possibility of such societies has led Snyder and others to consider watershed councils as a way of governing bioregions and ecosystems. Governance in the watershed begins with the grass roots (literally), the people, and their communities. People engage around their needs and the needs of the watershed. This approach acknowledges that what holds people together long enough to discover their power as citizens is their common inhabiting of a single place (Kemmis, 1990, pp. 118–120). Snyder says, "If the ground can become our common ground, we can begin to talk to each other (human and non-human) once again" (1992, p. 70). One of these watershed councils is the Yuba Watershed Institute in northern California.

Governments in California are beginning to embrace the concept too. In 1991 all state and federal agencies involved in resource management agreed on a memorandum of understanding to coordinate strategies to conserve biological diversity. This agreement encourages local agency staffs to help citizens form watershed councils as primary forums for resolution of local issues and conflicts related to biodiversity concerns. In one example, residents of San Juan Ridge are being asked by the U.S. Forest Service to help determine the future of the area's last old-growth forests. Nearby, in the Inimim Forest, the U.S. Bureau of Land Management and local residents are jointly creating a plan for forest management.

The memorandum of understanding recognizes the need to involve citizens in decisions that affect their homes, communities, and lands and to foster collaboration among state and federal agencies that share jurisdiction for a bioregion. It is the beginning of a renewed reliance on custom and consensus rather than rule-making and law. Snyder believes that "people are slowly coming to the realization that they can become members of the deep old biological communities of the land in a different kind of citizenship" (1992, p. 1).

In northwestern Montana, a similar bioregional approach to civics and citizenship is evolving, as we mentioned in an earlier chapter. Along the Clark Fork River, people have begun to see themselves not as residents of the region's towns and rural areas but as citizens of a place defined by the watershed. The Clark Fork Project, a group of citizens involving all the major stakeholders in the basin, came together in 1987 with the belief that the region's quality of life could be improved only by actively engaging inhabitants in meeting the challenges posed by the river basin. The intent of the Project is to improve the river and the lives of those who live there and to find a more cooperative, productive way for resolving disputes in the region. Rather than relying on governments and an adversarial system to solve problems, the stakeholders want to solve their problems themselves. Daniel Kemmis, one of the initiators of the project, calls this alternative a "citizenship" in which people "solve problems together, build trust, and then carry that trust into a new set of problems, and perhaps infect a new set of people with it" (1989, p. 5). Here citizens are coming together in ways that address problems on a scale congruent with the needs of the land and the people and that create a deeper, more intimate connection among citizens—a sense of belonging and community.

Becoming Our Own Moral Keepers

Our troubled history of racism and eugenics makes it very difficult to constructively address problems such as teen pregnancy and overpopulation, where some means of contraception is proposed as part of the solution. Cries of discrimination and genocide from minority citizens usually greet those who raise the issues, no matter how well-meaning they are. Public agencies, foundations, and nonprofit organizations are at loose ends when formulating social policies and programs in this area, because there is little agreement about ethically appropriate ways to support the use of contraceptive devices to address these problems.

When guidance is available, it has generally been developed by professional ethicists and is so abstruse or obscure that it has little meaning for the citizens and organizations that use or provide contraceptive products. In addition, ethicists often have an aura of moral authority—even arrogance—that makes their input sterile and distant; it is as if ordinary citizens were incapable of making informed moral judgments. For example, Dr. William C. DeVries, a well-known heart surgeon, told a *Louisville Courier-Journal* reporter that "the general society is not very well informed to make those decisions (as to the imposition of restraints on medical experiments on human patients), and that's why the medical society or the government who has a wider range of view comes in to make those decisions" (Berry, 1987, p. 120). And expert guidance too often fails to address the concerns of those most affected—the groups (predominately minority women, in the case of contraception) to which policies and programs are usually directed.

Confronted with these conflicts, the Hunt Alternatives Fund, a small Denver foundation, decided to take another approach to developing guidelines and strategies for the use of the surgically implanted contraceptive device Norplant. The Fund recognized that Norplant has one significant advantage over other contraceptive methods: it is effective for five years and thus eliminates the attention required in the use of other methods. The foundation wanted to provide equal access to contraceptive devices, especially Norplant, for all citizens regardless of financial circumstances. Rather than unilaterally beginning a program that would provide increased access to Norplant, the Fund decided to convene a group of citizens to decide on guidelines and strategies for Norplant's use. Half were women of color, since most contraceptive programs are directed largely at that population. Only in this way could the Fund be assured that the concerns and needs of those whose access to contraception is most difficult would be met in ethically appropriate ways.

The project added a more controversial twist in its approach to ethical issues when participants' experiences with contraception were accepted as legitimate information in the shaping of ethical guidelines. The idea of including people whose values are shaped by different experiences—and using these experiences to inform ethical decision making—is somehow foreign to many ethical experts. Most experts consider reason the only reliable standard for arriving at ethical decisions. Recently, one of the participants in the Norplant initiative suggested to a well-known ethical expert that ethical guidelines would be more valid if they were developed by groups that mirrored the ethnicity and experiences of the general population. The expert responded, "The quality and credibility of our work will be ensured more by the content and rigor of our arguments than by the characteristics of our working group." He failed to recognize that experiences as well as reason shape our values and the way we respond to ethical problems.

The group of twenty-five people (including twenty-one women) from throughout the community spent eight months working together. By creating a shared understanding about issues surrounding Norplant and by sharing their own experiences with contraception, the group learned to trust each other. Their experiences, regardless of an individual's race or culture, were accepted and legitimized by others. As one minority participant put it, they did not have to justify or rationalize their experiences, no matter how different or difficult. The real breakthrough came with the recognition that the sharing of a person's own experiences and stories is more valuable in reaching consensus than expert information is. That sharing allowed each of them to see a deeper human connection than the races, cultures, and interests they represented. Rather than a group of advocates of particular positions about contraception, they became a community of citizens addressing shared concerns.

There are now ethical guidelines for Norplant's (and, by extension, other contraceptive devices') use, as well as strategies for providing equal access to contraception for all citizens. The guidelines differ in a significant way from what might have come out of a group of professional ethicists: citizens from groups who will receive or benefit from Norplant have had a real say in decisions about how it is to be provided. Instead of relying on experts or intellectuals to be our moral keepers, the citizens themselves stepped into the role.

Conceiving a New Approach to
Legislation and Law-Making

Wick Sloane, a corporate strategies executive with Aetna Life & Casualty, chose a decidedly noncollaborative organization in which to try out some new ideas for working together—the Connecticut House of Representatives. In 1991 and 1992, the state's tax and funding issues had brought legislative action to a halt. Sloane had an idea for breaking the gridlock.

As a Fellow in Hartford's American Leadership Forum, Sloane had learned the techniques of collaborative leadership to deal with difficult community issues. He wanted to take these concepts into the legislative arena. He took his idea to Tom Ritter, another ALF graduate and chairman of the legislature's joint banking committee, to see if they could identify an issue where they could bring the issue's stakeholders together and reach agreement on appropriate responses. Frustrated by the gridlock, Ritter was eager to try a new approach: "Ninety-five percent of the legislators are smart and well-intentioned. Why can't we get things done?" (Condon, 1992, p. E3). The issue they chose was mortgage lending practices that discriminate against blacks and low-income urban residents. Part of Ritter's motivation was a desire to head off the bitter fights occurring in other state legislatures after the passage of the federal Home Mortgage Disclosure Act.

Instead of the usual nonproductive public hearings and destructive legislative battles that generally accompany such controversial issues, Sloane and Ritter created a supplementary process to bring together bankers, city and state officials, and neighborhood activists in a consensus-based problem-solving forum. Over several months of weekly meetings, the group learned skills for working together, built trust, gained a shared understanding of the problems, and identified more than twenty recommendations for improving minority lending practices. The result: new legislation—

quickly passed by both houses—governing bank practices for deny-ing mortgage loans and targeting several million dollars in new money for urban mortgages and programs to teach low-income res-idents how to establish credit histories. Ritter says, "It's a liberat-ing way to solve problems. People were working together, rather than at cross purposes" (Gurwitt, 1992, p. 17).

Sloane and Ritter believe that their success with the issue of minority lending practices will lead to acceptance by legislators of this unusual way to work with difficult issues. Ritter says of his col-leagues, "They don't understand the dynamic we created, but they do understand we accomplished something without all the turmoil and the yelling and screaming that usually happens" (Gurwitt, 1992, p. 18). Ritter, now speaker of the House, intends to take on a number of other legislative issues in this way. Perhaps even leg-islators can learn to collaborate.

Rethinking School Governance

In 1992 David Osborne and Ted Gaebler published their popular book *Reinventing Government: How the Entrepreneurial Spirit Is Transforming the Public Sector* (1992), about how government could become more responsive and consumer-driven. Following years of declining confidence in government, the ideas these men advo-cated were seen by many, both inside and outside of government, as the best means for restoring trust and confidence. Despite a grow-ing number of success stories in which these approaches were used, however, there is increasing sentiment that reinventing govern-ment in this fashion will not be enough to regain lost credibility. Simply making government more efficient and consumer-driven in delivering services ignores the desires of citizens to have a larger role in public life and to act as partners with government in addressing the needs of the community. Reinventing govern-ment—*governance* may be a more appropriate term—must go beyond more efficient and responsive service delivery; it must fundamentally change the relationship of citizens and government.

The fundamental assumptions about what government should do and the structures and practices of its institutions are rarely subject to question. As Robert Bellah notes, most people are not conscious of the beliefs and premises that underlie our system of government (Bellah and others, 1991, p. 19). Fewer still would be willing to question them, for fear of being criticized for demonstrating a "haughty contempt for the American institution of representative governance" (Peirce, 1992c, p. 2). When this kind of questioning of basic premises does occur, it usually begins with forces outside of the institution; those inside are too embedded in the assumptions to be aware of them or too unwilling to subject themselves to such penetrating scrutiny.

In New Orleans, a group of citizens frustrated by years of bickering, name-calling, and fraud among school board members formed the New Orleans School Board Forum's Coalition for Public Education (CPE) to press for reform of school governance. These citizens wanted to take advantage of the fact that in the 1992 election year, all seven school board seats would be open. Leslie Gerwin, executive director of the Metropolitan Area Committee Education Fund (MACEF) and the convener for the coalition, asserts that "the community had lost confidence in the school board and its ability to govern. We had the chance to really make a difference" ("New Orleans Fund . . . ," 1993, p. 3).

The first goal of CPE was to ensure that every stakeholder was at the table. "We made a tremendous effort to ensure that every group interested in public education was represented. MACEF's credibility in the community really helped to bring together all the different people" (p. 3), says Gerwin. Through a series of facilitated round-table discussions, the coalition reached a consensus about qualifications for effective school board membership. They created a questionnaire for candidates to find out about their policy and management goals and their perceptions about the board's proper role. The qualifications and the questionnaire became the starting point for media coverage and for organizing debates. CPE's purpose was not to endorse candidates but to ensure that voters could make informed decisions and to help increase voter turnout. The result was an election turnout more than twice the national average for school board elections and five new school board members and two reelected incumbents who met the criteria set by the coalition.

For many cities this would have been enough, but MACEF is now going further. Using the momentum and credibility gained in the election, MACEF is serving as a catalyst and a convener for a public dialogue about educational governance. In question will be the purpose, practices, and structure of school governance. Gerwin says, "Board members must develop their own vision, but their plans will not work if there is a mismatch with the community" ("New Orleans Fund . . . ," 1993, p. 9). By creating a constituency for change that can support elected leaders and overcome institutional barriers to change, MACEF hopes to create a new partnership of citizens and elected leaders that can restore confidence in the city's educational system. "It is a very unique opportunity for New Orleans," says Gerwin. "It's a chance for us to really address the problems we have been struggling with for years" (p. 9).

A Collaborative Approach to Urban Revitalization

In Atlanta, former President Jimmy Carter has started a major initiative to end poverty in the city. The Atlanta Project builds on Carter's "impossible dream" of bridging the gap between Atlanta's two cities—one rich and one poor. He wants to help in ways that recognize a role for all the city's citizens. "We ought to be helping but not in a supercilious 'I'm better than you' attitude," he says (Smothers, 1992, p. 5). He hopes to counter a public that has "run out of compassion." By bringing together local residents, government agencies, corporations, and nonprofits, the Atlanta Project seeks to create new partnerships that can revitalize the poor, mostly black inner-city neighborhoods. If it works, it will turn Atlanta's history of paternalistic leadership and exploitation of poor neighborhoods on its head and create an approach that can work in other poverty-stricken areas.

Unlike past government antipoverty programs, the Atlanta Project looks to neighborhood residents to make decisions about what they need. Building on the idea that the only consensus that really matters is that of the people who live in a place, twenty "cluster" groups have been created as forums for residents to determine needs and set priorities. The city's major corporations provide staff and resources to help the groups do their work. By becoming engaged around issues they care about, residents can begin to take control of their own future.

If successful, it will create a constituency for change that can force modifications in government bureaucracies. Columnist Neal Peirce wonders what will happen "when the newly empowered cluster task forces start to feel their oats and press for dramatic changes" in government services. "One can see," he says, "local political feathers flying" (1992a, p. 3).

The Atlanta Project is not without controversy. Carter has staked his immense credibility on its success, raising high expectations on the part of poor residents for quick results. Much of the initiating work was carried out by a small, exclusive group of people with little or no involvement of grass-roots representatives, bringing more charges of paternalism. Some minority representatives see the Project as another attempt to foist government and business responsibilities for social services onto hard-pressed local institutions (such as churches and neighborhood groups) and have declined to participate. Others say its leaders have been insensitive about racial issues.

If the Atlanta Project can overcome its rocky start—especially the resentment caused by the exclusive initiating group—it may offer new ideas for renewing poor, urban centers. Its reliance on cit-

izens rather than experts to determine needs and strategies marks
a turning point in how decisions affecting inner-city neighborhoods
are made. The Project builds on the competence and well-meaning motivation of the residents. Carter himself has learned to trust
poor people through his work with Habitat for Humanity. "We
worked side by side with them," he says, "and found them so eager,
ambitious and competent. . . . It is almost an impossible chasm for
some of us to cross, but with an adequate degree of groundwork and
acculturation it can be done" (Smothers, 1992, p. 5). The work of
the community is done by the community, not by outsiders. "The
theology of the Atlanta Project is building community," says Neil
Shorthouse, a member of the Project's steering group. "If we are
successful we will enable people to think differently about ways
they can share with each other" (Knack, 1993, p. 22).

Creating Civic Will

In every city and town in America, public opinion cries out for significant change on virtually every major community issue. In only
a few places, however, does the political or institutional will exist
to make any progress. Political leaders either fail to lead or cannot
lead because they are hamstrung by competing interest groups.
These leaders respond, citizens say, only to interest groups and
power players, both of whom are more interested in the negative
use of power—stopping others' actions that hurt them—than in
moving forward on the public's concerns. The focus of leadership
is on bringing together small groups of people or interest coalitions
to overpower others and achieve their ends. As power becomes
more fragmented, this becomes more difficult. When it works, it
leaves people divided. When it does not work, it leaves gridlock.
The link between public opinion and political will is broken.

Some places, though, are taking a different approach. In these
places, citizens and civic leaders recognize a missing link between

public opinion and political will—civic will. Rather than wasting time and energy on the futile hope of finding new and better candidates for office or on reforming electoral politics, some citizens and a few elected leaders are using collaborative approaches to create civic will. They understand that if the civic will exists, political and institutional will must follow. Just look at Citizens for Denver's Future, the Baltimore Commonwealth, and the New Orleans School Board Forum's Coalition for Public Education. In all three examples, political will resulted because there was a constituency for change—civic will—that could not be brushed aside by traditional political forces. Public policy problem solving and decision making shifted from politicians to citizens—people who got results by creating a new way of doing business around public issues.

The initiative for creating civic will can come from either "ordinary" citizens or elected leaders (or both). More than half of the collaborative initiatives we studied were begun by citizens who, frustrated by the failure of traditional politics, wanted to find more constructive ways to address public concerns. The motivation for elected leaders is similar. Frustrated and hamstrung by power players and interest groups in their attempts to lead, they look to citizens and civic will to overcome political gridlock and bureaucratic inertia. They understand that civic will is the force that can create and sustain needed change.

Civic will is also the way to sustain confidence in political leadership. This was recognized much earlier, in 1739, by the Marquis d'Argenson, one of the public servants of Louis XV, King of France. D'Argenson outlined a "royal democracy" that could overcome the resistance to reform of the country's hereditary nobility. He understood that "democracy is as much a friend of monarchy as the aristocracy is an enemy" (Schama, 1989, p. 113). This new kind of collective community—"a republic protected by a King"—would address the concerns of citizens while sustaining confidence in the monarchy. Unfortunately, his advice went unheeded and the citizens sent Louis XVI to the guillotine in 1793, when all faith in the monarchy disappeared in the French Revolution. In more recent times, U.S. citizens have lost confidence in political leaders who have attended primarily to an "aristocracy" of influence and interest. As a result, many of the country's best-known elected leaders have suffered similar, though less violent, fates.

Whether citizens or elected leaders, collaborative leaders operate from a very different premise than traditional leaders. Instead of pitting groups or coalitions against each other, they look to citizens for power and serve in a very different leadership role. Their operating premise is the collaborative premise: if you can bring the appropriate people together in constructive ways with good information, they will come up with good responses and get results. They trust their fellow citizens in the collaborative process when it is inclusive, constructive, and well informed. Their role is to convene, catalyze, and facilitate the work of others. They inspire people to act, help them solve problems as peers, build broad-based involvement, and sustain hope and participation. And they are unwilling to settle for *no* change. They know that the will to solve problems comes not from them or from elected leaders or "old boys" but from citizens engaged in addressing public issues. This new civic culture and the new kind of leadership that fosters it is overcoming the failures of traditional politics. Most significant, the new civic politics is solving problems, unifying communities, and engaging citizens when nothing else is working.

Building Community

One of the more important outcomes for people who engage collaboratively—and successfully—around an issue of shared concern is that stakeholders shift to broader, more inclusive perspectives; participants recognize that their well-being is intimately connected to the well-being of the community. Collaboration becomes more than a tactical or strategic means for resolving problems; it becomes a means of reestablishing oneself as a part of a larger community. It is this sense of connectedness arising out of engagement that is at the heart of successful collaboration. Others have spoken about it in many different ways under the rubric of "community."

Dictionaries fail to capture the deeper meaning of *community* as we are beginning to understand it. *Webster's Dictionary*, for example, defines it as people with common interests living in a particular area. This definition suggests little more than people who are affected by the same problems. There is no implication of an emotional tie or interdependent relationship among the people and their common interests. There is nothing about shared history or the stories that shape a local culture and bind it together. Another definition in *Webster's* says that community is a group of people—such as retired persons—with a common interest living together within a broader society. Here community defines a way of separating people around narrow interests, not bringing them together around broader interests, which should be its higher purpose. Taking *community* as a derivative of *commune*—to communicate intimately—implies a deeper connection and shared identity.

John Gardner, in *Building Community*, defines the role of community in this way: "Where community exists it confers upon its members identity, a sense of belonging, a measure of security. Individuals acquire a sense of self partly from their continuous relationships to others, and from the culture of their native place" (1991, p. 5). Gardner captures the dual purpose of community: to confirm self-identity and the sense of belonging to a larger group. And he warns of the dangers of exclusion, citing the destructiveness of cults, gangs, and other narrowly defined and dysfunctional communities. The Newark Collaboration Group's Maria Vizcarrondo-DeSoto says, "The greatest lesson I learned is to accept a definition of community that isn't limited to my own experience.

Everybody that interacts in my environment is part of the community. If you can accept that intellectually, spiritually, in your gut, you can bring people together."

Kentucky writer Wendell Berry describes the breakdown of community: "For example, when a community loses its memory, its members no longer know one another. How can they know one another if they have forgotten or have never learned one another's stories? If they do not know one another's stories, how can they know whether or not to trust one another? People who do not trust one another do not help one another, and moreover they fear one another. And this is our predicament now. Because of a general distrust and suspicion, we not only lose one another's help and companionship, but we are all now living in jeopardy of being sued" (1990, p. 157). So to have a sense of community, we have to know each other's stories—not necessarily have the same experiences—in order to trust each other. Bob Keller of the Baltimore Commonwealth tells a story: "We at one time shared our visions with one another. We had corporate guys looking black ministers in the eye and saying, 'I'm afraid.' It took us five years to get to that point. That was magical. It was about shared values, visions, and stories." "A good community," Berry says, "insures itself by trust, by good faith and good will, by mutual help" (p. 158).

Amitai Etzioni, one of the founders of the Communitarian movement, comes at community in a different way: "We were troubled by the finding that many Americans are rather reluctant to accept responsibilities. We were distressed that many Americans are all too eager to spell out what they are entitled to but are all too slow to give something back to others and to the community. We adopted the name *Communitarian* to emphasize that the time had come to attend to our responsibilities to the conditions and elements we all share, to the community" (1993, p. 15). He asks us to shift our perspective from narrow, parochial interests to a broader perspective and to recognize the need to speak for that larger perspective. He does not suggest the giving up of individual rights but instead the recognition of the dependence of the success of individuals on the health of the larger community and our responsibility for ensuring that health.

Sociologist Robert Bellah and his colleagues present one more aspect of community that needs to be considered: "People growing up in communities of memory not only hear the stories that tell how the community came to be, what its hopes and fears are, and how its ideals are exemplified in outstanding men and women; they also participate in the practices—ritual, aesthetic, ethical—that define the community as a way of life. We call these 'practices of commitment' for they define the patterns of loyalty and obligation that keep the community alive" (Bellah and others, 1985). Communities have practices that create shared stories—a community of memory—and rituals that allow stories to be told. These practices create the culture of the community.

We can take these as necessary elements of community. Members are confirmed in their individual identities and have a sense of belonging to and inclusion in the larger community. They trust each other because they know each other's stories; and since they trust each other, they can be of mutual help. They acknowledge and act on their responsibility to the broader community and recognize their interdependence with each other. They have practices—rituals, ways of working together, and so on—that allow them to engage successfully around issues of shared concern. These practices create history and define the culture of the community. Successful collaboration, as we have understood it, creates these necessary elements.

A Legacy of Hope

The challenges facing U.S. cities and regions cannot be addressed through a fruitless politics of advocacy that leaves us in despair and without hope. Our ability to create healthier communities, become better people, and live together more peacefully depends on our willingness to work and act together. It depends also on our capacity to imagine new and constructive ways for coming together across lines of difference and engaging in the difficult—yet demonstrably possible—task of defining shared visions and strategies that get results. In our research, we have seen the emergence of a new vision of leadership that can bring us together, help us focus on our shared concerns, and keep us engaged. We have seen the possibility of building, through personal engagement with others in a given place, a deeper sense of shared responsibility for our collective future. We have seen a restoration of hope that we can create or revitalize and nurture deeply connecting and effective communities. And we understand the source of this renewing force: anyone—whether citizen or civic leader—who cares deeply enough to engage fellow citizens in the difficult but deeply satisfying work of collaboratively addressing the shared concerns of the community.

Appendixes

Appendixes

The Research

An advisory board helped us design this research project. Its members gave us orientation, suggestions, and guidance in the early stages. They reviewed our progress with us and helped us make appropriate adjustments in the middle stages. They critiqued our results and helped us refine our conclusions in the final stages. They are an extraordinarily competent and knowledgeable group of individuals. With apologies for brevity, we introduce them here:

- Ambassador Harlan Cleveland, dean (retired), Hubert H. Humphrey Institute of Public Affairs, University of Minnesota
- Ronald A. Heifetz, M.D., lecturer in public policy, John F. Kennedy School of Government, Harvard University
- Barbara Kellerman, Ph.D., former dean of graduate studies, Fairleigh Dickinson University, and visiting professor, George Washington University
- William McGill, Ph.D., former president of Columbia University, professor of psychology, University of California, San Diego
- John Parr, president, National Civic League
- Elsa A. Porter, Washington, D.C.–based leadership consultant and former assistant secretary of commerce in the Carter Administration

The research itself took three years and was organized around two phases.

Phase 1: An Analysis of Successful Collaborative Efforts

Phase 1 was designed to produce some tentative conclusions, or hypotheses, about the nature of successful collaboration. These hypotheses would be based upon detailed analyses of a small set of carefully selected cases. These hypotheses could then be tested on a larger and more diverse sample of cases (in Phase 2 of the research).

The criteria for selecting the cases, given also in Chapter Three, were these:

- The collaboration produced concrete, tangible results. That is, a fundamental impact on the root cause of a problem or situation was made; the effort generated more than simply a set of activities or some structure building devoid of real impact on the problem.

- The problem was sufficiently complex that collaboration across sector lines in the community was necessary in order to impact the problem or condition.

- Significant barriers/obstacles existed that had to be overcome in addressing the issue.

- There were many and diverse stakeholders involved in the issue. It was not simply a collaboration of vested interests but addressed concerns of the community as a whole.

- There was widespread acknowledgment and recognition of the collaboration's success in dealing with the issue.

The cases selected that met these criteria were the Phoenix

Futures Forum, the Baltimore Commonwealth, the Newark Collaboration Group, Citizens for Denver's Future, Roanoke Vision, and the American Leadership Forum. The data generated from these cases were predominantly qualitative. The main source of information was the fifteen to twenty interviews we conducted for each case. Most of the interviews were done with stakeholders—the people from a variety of community sectors who were involved in and responsible for the success of the collaborative effort. However, a second kind of person was also interviewed for each case: "observers." These were people outside the case—not directly involved, not stakeholders—but they were knowledgeable about the community in general and about the case in particular. More often than not, these observers were newspaper columnists or reporters, television reporters, or experts from local academic institutions.

The analyses of the cases given were pretty wide-ranging. In the interviews, we asked about the nature of the problem, its background and history, and any factors that were relevant to the timing of the collaborative effort. We asked about the stakeholders—who they were, what interests they represented, whether they had had any prior history of relationship with each other, how they perceived the problem similarly or differently, and so on. We investigated the results of the project, asking about such things as what outcomes had been produced by it and what side effects were discernible from it. We asked about the obstacles that were encountered during the course of the project and how these obstacles were overcome. We wanted to know whether or not the participants and the observers considered the project successful, and to what degree. We were interested in the reasons people offered for the success of the project and the main lessons they had learned from the project. We asked them to recall and describe points in time when the project was going especially well or especially poorly and to tell us what was happening at those points in time. We asked about the values, cultures, and qualities of the community that impacted the project. And we asked the interviewees to tell us what we had overlooked, or what our questions had missed, that we needed to know about in order to really understand the project and why it had gone the way it had.

The interviews were supplemented by other sources of information. Records of meetings, preliminary and final reports, newsletters and other correspondence, media reports, editorials, and commentaries—though the primary analysis remained focused on the interviews.

The interviews were tape-recorded and transcribed. The transcripts of each case were analyzed to identify the characteristics commonly attributed to the case by the interviewees. The characteristics of the individual cases were then compared across the six cases in order to identify a preliminary set of "characteristics of successful collaboration." (Remember that this first phase of the research was designed to produce a set of preliminary hypotheses about successful collaboration that would then be tested on a later, larger sample of cases. Therefore, our analysis retained any plausible explanation for the success of an individual case and any characteristic that occurred in at least two cases. We did not want to overlook anything.)

We ended Phase 1 with a preliminary set of hypotheses. These hypotheses fell into three broad categories:

- *Context.* The kinds of problems faced, the conditions surrounding the collaborative effort, the broader context within which collaboration is more likely to succeed
- *Results.* The tangible results of the collaborative effort, the less concrete results, and some noteworthy side effects associated with these cases
- *Process.* How it was done and what emerged as explanations or reasons for its success

Many reasonable hypotheses emerged from the first six cases.

As we began Phase 2, we confronted several questions: Which hypotheses would be retained? Which explanations should be believed? Which characteristics are more frequently present in successful collaboration? In what concepts or principles should we be most confident?

Phase 2: Discovering the Essential Features of Successful Collaboration

In order to test the hypotheses that grew from Phase 1 of the research, forty-six additional cases were selected. Like the initial cases, these cases were selected with the assistance of the National Civic League. The cases were these:

1. Economic Development Task Force; Shasta/Redding Counties, California
2. Charlotte-Mecklenburg Citizen Forum; Charlotte, North Carolina
3. Atlanta Historic Preservation Program; Atlanta, Georgia
4. Greater Indianapolis Progress Committee; Indianapolis, Indiana
5. Greater Cleveland Roundtable Racial Unity Program; Cleveland, Ohio
6. Transportation 2000; Santa Clara County, California
7. Boise Clean Air Program; Boise, Idaho
8. Community Development Strategy Group and Neighborhood Progress Inc.; Cleveland, Ohio
9. Culture of Poverty Think Tank; Shelby County, Tennessee
10. Swinomish/Skagit Agreement; Seattle, Washington
11. Oak Park Mall; Chicago, Illinois
12. Challenge 95; Miami Valley Region, Ohio

13. Caring for Kids; Jacksonville, Florida
14. Citizens' Goals 2000; Colorado Springs, Colorado
15. Municipal League of Seattle and King County; Seattle, Washington
16. Toward 2007: Designing Our Future; James City County, Virginia
17. Central Oregon Regional Strategy; Central Oregon
18. Wenatchee Community Resource Center; Wenatchee, Washington
19. Community and Resource Exchange; Minneapolis and Hennepin County, Minnesota
20. Springdale West Pilot Project; Long Beach, California
21. Joint Venture Between Seneca Indian Nation and the City of Salamanca; Salamanca, New York
22. Lincoln Waste Utilization Plant; Lincoln, Nebraska
23. Lincoln/Lancaster Star Venture; Lincoln, Nebraska
24. Bay Vision 20/20; San Francisco, California
25. Jobs for the Future; Bridgeport, Connecticut
26. Dallas Citizens' Council; Dallas, Texas
27. Confluence, St. Louis; St. Louis, Missouri
28. Greater Philadelphia Urban Affairs Coalition; Philadelphia, Pennsylvania
29. Mobile United; Mobile, Alabama
30. Gaithersburg Homeless Program; Gaithersburg, Maryland
31. Kansas City Consensus; Kansas City, Missouri
32. Corporation for Effective Government; Toledo, Ohio
33. Jacksonville Community Council; Jacksonville, Florida
34. Chelan Water Agreement; State of Washington
35. Citizens' League of Cleveland; Cleveland, Ohio
36. Chattanooga Venture; Chattanooga, Tennessee
37. I-30 Working Group; Fort Worth, Texas
38. Bellevue Against Drugs; Macon, Georgia
39. Consensus Building Workshops on the Regional Land Use

Plan; Lake Tahoe, California and Nevada
40. Empowering the Vision; Rock Hill, South Carolina
41. Community Action Group; Winston-Salem, North Carolina
42. General Plan Update; Santa Barbara, California
43. Abilene Choosing Tomorrow—Now!; Abilene, Texas
44. Savannah/Chatham Vision 20/20; Savannah and Chatham Counties, Georgia
45. Community Unity Forum; Mohave County, Arizona
46. Comprehensive Plan Update; Hampton, Virginia

For each Phase 2 follow-up with these additional cases, two knowledgeable respondents were identified and interviewed by phone. In the phone interviews, we described each of the characteristics present in each preliminary hypothesis and asked the respondent whether or not that characteristic was present in the collaboration case he or she was being asked about. The use of two respondents per case allowed for testing the hypotheses with independent respondents, both describing the same case.

The data from these interviews were statistically analyzed. Specific characteristics of effective collaboration were confirmed when they were present a statistically significant number of times in the forty-six cases.

Appendix B

Assessing Collaboration

This appendix contains a measurement device for assessing the status of a collaborative effort. This device is included for two reasons:

1. It may serve as a feedback strategy whereby members of a collaborative group can describe the group, obtain a sense of how well the group is doing, and uncover for discussion issues related to improving the collaboration process.
2. It may serve as an instrument for research—an additional avenue for understanding collaboration and the factors that contribute to its success.

The instrument, "Working Together: A Profile of Collaboration," grew partly out of the research reported in this book. It assesses five dimensions of collaboration:

1. The context for the collaborative group
2. The structure or design of the collaboration
3. The members' skills and attitudes
4. The process that is being used
5. The results that are being accomplished

Twenty-three collaborative groups have been assessed with this instrument as of this writing. The early results suggest reasonable reliability and validity for the measure. Cronbach's alpha (a reliability index) for the five dimensions is as follows: .463, .769, .869, .851, and .799 respectively. The low alpha for Dimension 1 (context) comes from very little variance on the item scores. That is, *everyone* has reported a high sense of urgency about the problem being addressed by the collaborative group.

Preliminary validity results are encouraging. The instrument is sensitive to, and discriminates among, many features of the collaboration, including urban versus rural groups and general policy versus individual case decisions. But more important, the instrument has been shown to correlate significantly with success in achieving the actual, concrete results (such as reducing the number of youths held in detention facilities) sought by the collaborative efforts (Tjaden, 1993).

The research with this instrument, as well as the data base being maintained on collaborative groups, is in an early stage. The instrument's inclusion here is based on the hope that others will use it and contribute to the emerging data base and that our understanding of collaboration will thereby continue to grow.

Working Together:
A Profile of Collaboration

The purpose of this questionnaire is to record your opinions about items that measure collaboration effectiveness. Your honest responses to these items will be extremely helpful. Your responses will be statistically summarized and displayed, along with the responses of others, without identifying you individually.

Collaboration Identification:

You are a member of a group. The group may be called a partnership, consortium, or coalition. The group exists to deal with one or more concerns, issues, or goals. The name of the group is below. You will be asked to report the extent to which certain items are true or not true of your group. As you respond to each of the items in this questionnaire, please keep in mind the group you are describing.

NAME OF THE GROUP:

_____

Instructions:

Items are grouped into five categories. To the left of each item is a scale for recording your responses. Read the item, think about the extent to which it describes your group, and fill in the appropriate circle.

True	More True Than False	More False Than True	False	

The Context of the Collaboration

○	○	○	○	1. Now is a good time to address the issue about which we are collaborating.
○	○	○	○	2. Our collaborative effort was started because certain individuals wanted to do something about this issue.
○	○	○	○	3. The situation is so critical, we must act now.

True	More True Than False	More False Than True	False	
				The Structure of the Collaboration
O	O	O	O	4. Our collaboration has access to credible information that supports problem solving and decision making.
O	O	O	O	5. Our group has access to the expertise necessary for effective meetings.
O	O	O	O	6. We have adequate physical facilities to support the collaborative efforts of the group and its subcommittees.
O	O	O	O	7. We have adequate staff assistance to plan and administer the collaborative effort.
O	O	O	O	8. The membership of our group includes those stakeholders affected by the issue.
O	O	O	O	9. Our membership is not dominated by any one group or sector.
O	O	O	O	10. Stakeholders have agreed to work together on this issue.
O	O	O	O	11. Stakeholders have agreed on what decisions will be made by the group.
O	O	O	O	12. Our group has set ground rules and norms about how we will work together.
O	O	O	O	13. We have a method for communicating the activities and decisions of the group to all members.
O	O	O	O	14. Our collaboration is organized in working subgroups when necessary to attend to key performance areas.
O	O	O	O	15. There are clearly defined roles for group members.

True	More True Than False	More False Than True	False	
				Collaboration Members
○	○	○	○	16. Members are more interested in getting a good group decision than improving the position of their home organization.
○	○	○	○	17. Members are willing to let go of an idea for one that appears to have more merit.
○	○	○	○	18. Members have the communication skills necessary to help the group progress.
○	○	○	○	19. Members of the collaboration balance task and social needs so that the group can work comfortably and productively.
○	○	○	○	20. Members are effective liaisons between their home organizations and the group.
○	○	○	○	21. Members are willing to devote whatever effort is necessary to achieve the goals.
○	○	○	○	22. Members monitor the effectiveness of the process.
○	○	○	○	23. Members trust each other sufficiently to honestly and accurately share information, perceptions, and feedback.

True	More True Than False	More False Than True	False	
				## The Collaboration Process
O	O	O	O	24. We frequently discuss how we are working together.
O	O	O	O	25. Divergent opinions are expressed and listened to.
O	O	O	O	26. The process we are engaged in is likely to have a real impact on the problem.
O	O	O	O	27. We have an effective decision-making process.
O	O	O	O	28. The openness and credibility of the process help members set aside doubts or skepticism.
O	O	O	O	29. There are strong, recognized leaders who support this collaborative effort.
O	O	O	O	30. Those who are in positions of power or authority are willing to go along with our decisions or recommendations.
O	O	O	O	31. We set aside vested interests to achieve our common goal.
O	O	O	O	32. We have a strong concern for preserving a credible, open process.
O	O	O	O	33. We are inspired to be action-oriented.
O	O	O	O	34. We celebrate our group's successes as we move toward achieving the final goal.

True	More True Than False	More False Than True	False	

The Results of the Collaboration

O	O	O	O	35. We have concrete, measurable goals to judge the success of our collaboration.
O	O	O	O	36. We have identified interim goals to maintain the group's momentum.
O	O	O	O	37. There is an established method for monitoring performance and providing feedback on goal attainment.
O	O	O	O	38. Our group is effective in obtaining the resources it needs to accomplish its objectives.
O	O	O	O	39. Our group is willing to confront and resolve performance issues.
O	O	O	O	40. The time and effort of the collaboration are directed at obtaining the goals rather than keeping the collaboration in business.

What one change would most improve the effectiveness of this collaborative effort?

If you would like information on the theory, scoring, or norms for "Working Together: A Profile of Collaboration," contact:
OMNI Research and Training, Inc.
2329 West Main St. #330
Littleton, CO 80120–1951
(303) 797–2633
800–279–2070
FAX (303) 797–2660

References

Alinsky, S. *Rules for Radicals*. New York: Vintage Books, 1971.

"America's Blacks." *Economist*, Mar. 30, 1991, pp. 17–21.

Anderson, E., and Gavin, J. "Lawmakers Compromise on Schools." *Denver Post*, May 7, 1992, p. 1.

Barron, J. "A Livable City? Newark. Yes, Newark." *New York Times*, June 18, 1991, p. B1.

Bellah, R., and others. *Habits of the Heart*. Berkeley: University of California Press, 1985.

Bellah, R., and others. *The Good Society*. New York: Knopf, 1991.

Bennis, W., and Nanus, B. *Leaders: The Strategies for Taking Charge*. New York: HarperCollins, 1985.

Berry, W. "Men and Women in Search of Common Ground." *Home Economics*. San Francisco: Northpoint Press, 1987.

Berry, W. "The Work of Local Culture." In W. Berry, *What Are People For?* San Francisco: Northpoint Press, 1990.

Burns, J. *Leadership*. New York: HarperCollins, 1978.

Byrne, J. "Management's New Gurus." *Business Week*, Aug. 31, 1992, p. 44.

Byrne, J., Brandt, R., and Port, O. "The Virtual Corporation." *Business Week*, Feb. 8, 1993, p. 99.

"Choices for Colorado's Future." Denver: The Colorado Trust, 1992.

Cleveland, H. "The Management of Peace." *G.A.O. Journal*, Winter 1990–1991, pp. 4–23.

Coleman, J. "The Dynamics of Community Controversy." In R. Warren and L. Lyon (eds.), *New Perspectives on the American Community*. (5th ed.) Chicago: Dorsey Press, 1989.

Condon, T. "The Consensus: A Stalled City Needs Vision and Action." *Hartford Courant: A Special Report*, Mar. 1991a, p. 2.

Condon, T. "Underneath the Gloom, a City with a Lot Going for It." *Hartford Courant: A Special Report*, Mar. 1991b, p. 10.

Condon, T. "Old-Fashioned Advice: Listen and Negotiate." *Hartford Courant*, Jan. 26, 1992, p. E3.

"Creating Healthier Communities." *Healthier Communities Action Kit* (Module 2). San Francisco: Healthcare Forum, 1993.

Deming, W. *Out of the Crisis*. Cambridge, Mass.: MIT Press, 1986.

Diegmueller, K. "Associations Try to Be 'All Things to All People.'" *Education Week*, Apr. 29, 1992, p. 8.

D'Souza, D. *Illiberal Education*. New York: Free Press, 1991.

Duhl L. "Healthy Cities: Myth or Reality?" In J. Ashton (ed.), *Healthy Cities*. Milton Keynes, England: Open University Press, 1992.

Etzioni, A. *The Spirit of Community*. New York: Crown, 1993.

Farkas, S. *Divided Within, Besieged Without: The Politics of Education in Four American School Districts*. New York: Public Agenda Foundation, 1993.

Fullan, M., and Miles, M. "Getting Reform Right." *Phi Delta Kappan*, June 1992, p. 752.

Gallup International Institute. *America's Cities and Communities: Problems and People Power*. Denver: National Civic League, 1990.

Gardner, J. *Leadership: A Sampler of the Wisdom of John Gardner*. Minneapolis: University of Minnesota Press, 1981.

Gardner, J. *Building Community*. Washington, D.C.: Independent Sector, 1991.

Gates, C. "Making a Case for Collaborative Problem Solving." *National Civic Review*, Spring 1991, pp. 113–119.

Germer, F. "School Fund Stalemate Disgusts Legislators." *Rocky Mountain News*, Mar. 24, 1992, p. 9.

Goldberg, A., and Larson, C. *Successful Communication and Negotiation*. Gardena, Calif.: International Right of Way Association, 1992.

Goodlad, J. *Teachers for Our Nation's Schools*. San Francisco: Jossey-Bass, 1990.

Gray, B. *Collaborating: Finding Common Ground for Multiparty Problems*. San Francisco: Jossey-Bass, 1989.

Greenleaf, R. *Servant Leadership*. New York: Paulist Press, 1977.

Greider, W. *Who Will Tell the People?* New York: Basic Books, 1992.

Gurwitt, R. "Resolving Issues Without Tears." *Governing*, May 1992, pp. 17–18.

Hall, J., and Weschler, L. "The Phoenix Futures Forum: Creating Vision, Implanting Community." *National Civic Review*, Spring 1991, pp. 135–157.

Harwood, R. *Citizens and Politics: The View from Main Street America*. Dayton, Ohio: Kettering Foundation, 1991.

Heifetz, R., and Sinder, R. "Political Leadership: Managing the Public's Problem Solving." In R. Reich (ed.), *The Power of Public Ideas*. New York: Ballinger, 1988.

Kemmis, D. "The Art of the Possible in the Home of Hope." *Northern Lights*, Fall 1988, pp. 9–18.

Kemmis, D. "The Miner's Canary." *Northern Lights*, Spring 1989, pp. 3–5.

Kemmis, D. *Community and the Politics of Place*. Norman: University of Oklahoma Press, 1990.

Kemmis, D. "What We Make of It." *Northern Lights*, 1992, 8(2), 23.

Knack, R. "Empowerment to the People." *Planning*, Feb. 1993, p. 22.

Kotter, J. *A Force for Change: How Leadership Differs from Management*. New York: Free Press, 1990.

Kouzes, J., and Posner, B. *The Leadership Challenge: How to Get Extraordinary Things Done in Organizations.* San Francisco: Jossey-Bass, 1987.

Larson, C., and LaFasto, F. *Teamwork: What Must Go Right/What Can Go Wrong.* Newbury Park, Calif.: Sage, 1989.

Logsdon, J. "Interests and Interdependence in the Formation of Social Problem-Solving Collaborations." *Journal of Applied Behavior Science*, 1991, 27(2), 23–37.

Machiavelli, N. *The Prince.* Chicago: University of Chicago Press, 1985. (Originally published 1532.)

Mattessich, P., and Monsey, B. *Collaboration: What Makes It Work.* St. Paul, Minn.: Wilder Foundation, 1992.

Mead, L. "Job Programs and Other Bromides." *New York Times*, May 19, 1992, p. A23.

Melaville, A., and Blank, M. *Together We Can.* Washington, D.C.: U.S. Government Printing Office, 1993.

Michael, D. "Leadership's Shadow: The Dilemma of Denial." *Futures*, Jan./Feb. 1991, p. 69.

Mouat, L. "Newark Experiences Renaissance." *Christian Science Monitor*, July 10, 1991, p. 8.

"New Orleans Fund Ends Blame and Shame, Launches New Era of Governance." *Connections* (publication of the Public Education Fund Network), Spring 1993, pp. 3–9.

"Next Century Newark." *New York Times*, Sept. 20, 1986, p. 26.

Nielsen, P. "The State of the Clark Fork." *Northern Lights*, Spring 1989, p. 11.

Nieves, E. "U.S. Refuses to Supervise Newark Job." *New York Times*, Feb. 22, 1992, p. 28.

Oka, T. "Cleveland Mayor Tells Story of City's Rebound." *Christian Science Monitor*, Aug. 12, 1991, p. 9.

Oreskes, M. "American Politics Faltering as U.S. Vision Changes the World." *New York Times*, Mar. 18, 1990, p. A22.

Osborne, D., and Gaebler, T. *Reinventing Government: How the Entrepreneurial Spirit Is Transforming the Public Sector.* Reading, Mass.: Addison-Wesley, 1992.

Owens, A., and Kennedy, C. *A School District in Transition.* Denver: Citizens for Quality Schools, 1992.

Peirce, N. "Can Carter's 'Atlanta Project' Become an 'America Project'?" *Washington Post Writers Group*, Oct. 18, 1992a, p. 3.

Peirce, N. "Oregon Charge: A Health Care 'amBush.'" *Washington Post Writers Group*, Aug. 16, 1992b, p. 2.

Peirce, N. "School Boards: Ripe for Overhaul?" *Washington Post Writers Group*, Apr. 26, 1992c, p. 2.

Peirce, N. *Citistates.* Washington, D.C.: Seven Locks Press, 1993.

Perlez, J. "Monitoring Vital Signs in Newark," *New York Times*, Oct. 20, 1985, p. E6.

Putnam, R. *Making Democracy Work: Civic Traditions in Modern Italy.* Princeton: Princeton University Press, 1993.

Reich, R. "The Secession of the Successful." *New York Times Magazine*, Jan. 20, 1991, p. 16.

Rilke, R. *Letters to a Young Poet.* New York: Vintage Books, 1984. (Originally published 1908.)

Roberts, N., and Bradley, R. "Stakeholder Collaboration and Innovation: A Study of Public Policy Initiation at the State Level." *Journal of Applied Behavioral Science*, 1991, *27*(2), 209–227.

Roberts, S. "Newark's Loss May Really Be Its Renaissance." *New York Times*, Apr. 8, 1991, p. B1.

Schama, S. *Citizens: A Chronicle of the French Revolution.* New York: Vintage Books, 1989.

Schlesinger, A. Jr. *The Disuniting of America.* Knoxville, Tenn.: Whittle Direct Books, 1991.

Smothers, R. "Carter's Civic Crusade Tries to Meld Two Atlantas." *New York Times*, Apr. 11, 1992, p. 5.

Snyder, G. "The Etiquette of Freedom." In G. Snyder, *The Practice of the Wild.* San Francisco: Northpoint Press, 1990.

Snyder, G. "Coming into the Watershed." *Wild Earth: Special Issue*, 1992, pp. 65–70.

Steel, R. *Walter Lippmann and the American Century.* New York: Random House, 1980.

Sweeney, C. "Teamwork and Collaboration in Volunteer Groups with Extraordinary and Ordinary Outcomes." Unpublished doctoral dissertation, Department of Human Communication Studies, University of Denver, 1990.

Tjaden, C. *Using 'Working Together: A Profile for Collaboration' to Analyze Systems Change.* Littleton, Colo.: Learning Profiles, 1993.

Traver, N. "Why Washington Doesn't Work." *Time*, Apr. 8, 1992, p. 20.

Turque, B. "Reversal of Fortune." *Newsweek*, Sept. 9, 1991, pp. 44–45.

Underdue, T. "Newark Puts 'Collective' Foot Forward to Win All-America City Award." *Newark Star-Ledger*, June 17, 1991, p. N1.

Walton, M. *Deming Management at Work.* New York: Perigee Books, 1991.

Westbrook, R. *John Dewey and American Democracy.* Ithaca, N.Y.: Cornell University Press, 1991.

Wood, D., and Gray, B. "Toward a Comprehensive Theory of Collaboration." *Journal of Applied Behavioral Science*, 1991, *27*(2), 139–162.

Index